Writing Essays

How to plan, draft, and revise,

Viva Studymates

Writing Essays

How to plan, draft, and revise,

2nd edition

Derek Soles Ph.D
Drexel University, Philadelphia

Viva Books Private Limited
New Delhi • Mumbai • Chennai • Kolkata • Bangalore • Hyderabad

First Indian Edition 2007

VIVA BOOKS PRIVATE LIMITED

- 4737/23 Ansari Road, Daryaganj, New Delhi 110 002
  E-mail: vivadelhi@vivagroupindia.net, Tel. 42242200
- Plot No. 76, Service Industries, Shirvane, Sector 1, Nerul, Navi Mumbai 400 706
  E-mail: vivamumbai@vivagroupindia.net, Tel. 27721273, 27721274
- Jamals Fazal Chambers, 26 Greams Road, Chennai 600 006
  E-mail: vivachennai@vivagroupindia.net, Tel. 28290304, 28294241
- B-103, Jindal Towers, 21/1A/3 Darga Road, Kolkata 700 017
  E-mail: vivakolkata@vivagroupindia.net, Tel. 22836381, 22816713
- 7, Sovereign Park Apartments, 56-58, K. R. Road, Basavanagudi, Bangalore 560 004
  E-mail: vivabangalore@vivagroupindia.net, Tel. 26607409, 26607410
- 101-102 Mughal Marc Apartments, 3-4-637 to 641, Narayanguda, Hyderabad 500 029
  E-mail: vivahyderabad@vivagroupindia.net, Tel. 27564481, 27564482

Published by arrangement with

Studymates Limited
PO Box 2,
Bishops Lydeard,
Somerset TA4 3YE,
United Kingdom,

ISBN 81-309-0717-8

Published by Vinod Vasishtha for Viva Books Private Limited, 4737/23 Ansari Road
New Delhi-110 002. Printed and bound at Anand Sons, Delhi-110 092.

Contents

Preface to the Second Edition ix

1 Getting Started 1

One-minute overview 1
Considering your reader 1
Establishing your purpose 4
Thinking about your topic 7
Composing your thesis statement 9
A case study 10
Tutorial 13

2 Researching Your Topic 15

One-minute overview 15
Finding the right books 15
Checking periodicals 17
Searching the Internet 18
Consulting your librarian 19
Our case study continued 19
Tutorial 22

3 How to Make a Plan 23

One-minute overview 23
Planning an informative essay 23
Planning a compare/contrast essay 25
Planning a persuasive essay 27
Our case study continued 30
Tutorial 32

4 Analysing and Interpreting Information 33

One-minute overview 33
Defining the distinguishing features of the whole 34
Dividing the whole into its component parts and analysing the parts 34
Interpreting the relationship of the parts to the whole 36
Learning how to analyse and interpret 36
Tutorial 38

5 Writing a Clear and Specific Opening 39

One-minute overview 39
Sample introductory paragraph 1 39
Sample introductory paragraph 2 40

Sample introductory paragraph 3 41
Sample introductory paragraph 4 41
Sample introductory paragraph 5 42
Our case study continued 43
Tutorial 44

6 Writing Complete Body Paragraphs 46

One-minute overview 46
Composing a topic sentence 46
Developing your topic sentence 47
Maintaining paragraph unity 47
Sample body paragraphs 48
Our case study continued 52
Tutorial 55

7 Writing an Explicit Conclusion 58

One-minute overview 58
Sample concluding paragraph 1 58
Sample concluding paragraph 2 59
Sample concluding paragraph 3 60
Sample concluding paragraph 4 61
Sample concluding paragraph 5 62
Our case study continued 62
Tutorial 63

8 Using Cohesive Ties between Sentences and Paragraphs 65

One-minute overview 65
Using transitional words and phrases 65
Using repetition 66
Using substitution 67
Our case study continued 68
Tutorial 70

9 Avoiding Errors in Sentence Grammar 72

One-minute overview 72
Pronoun case 72
Pronoun reference 75
Verb tense and mood 76
Subject–verb agreement 79
Tutorial 80

10 Avoiding Errors in Sentence Structure 84

One-minute overview 84
Sentence fragments 84
The run-on sentence 87
Misplaced and dangling modifiers 89

Faulty parallelism	91
Wordiness	92
Tutorial	94
11 Writing with Style	**99**
One-minute overview	99
Using subordination	99
Effective parallelism	102
Using word order effectively	104
Tutorial	105
12 Punctuating Your Sentences Correctly	**109**
One-minute overview	109
Punctuation at the end of a sentence	109
Punctuation within a sentence	110
Punctuation within a word	117
Tutorial	120
13 Choosing the Best Words	**124**
One-minute overview	124
Establishing context	124
Determining the meaning	125
Choosing the right voice	127
An example	128
Our case study continued	130
Audrey's essay	130
Tutorial	136
14 Acknowledging Your Sources Accurately and Completely	**138**
One-minute overview	138
Footnotes	139
The References List at the end of the essay	141
Our case study continued	143
Tutorial	145
Websites for Student Writers	**147**
Index	**149**

Preface to the Second Edition

To succeed in your school, college and university courses, you will be required to write many essays. Writing an essay is a demanding intellectual activity. You must read books and journal articles about your topic and surf the net for the best electronic sources, making careful and detailed notes as you proceed. You must analyse and synthesise these notes and from them develop a plan to guide you as you draft the paragraphs that will comprise your essay. You must write and revise your work, checking to make certain you are providing your readers with the detailed, authoritative information they expect. You must go through your paper yet again, this time proofreading and editing, correcting those errors in grammar, sentence structure, spelling and punctuation that can mar an otherwise solid effort.

As if all of this were not challenge enough, you then must pass all of your hard work to someone who probably knows even more than you do about the subject of your essay and about how to express that knowledge clearly, persuasively and forcefully. Finally you must wait while that person judges the quality of your essay and assigns to it a value, in relation to the value of similar essays written by your classmates.

The book you are holding, *Writing Essays: How to plan, draft, write and revise,* will help you meet this challenge confidently and successfully. It is what you need to succeed at school and college: a step-by-step guide to writing excellent academic essays. The first four chapters explain how to gather, evaluate, organise, analyse and synthesise the information you will need to provide content for your essay. Chapters 5–7 explain how to write effective introductory, body and concluding paragraphs for essays. Chapters 8–13 teach you how to revise and edit your work, to correct errors in grammar, sentence structure and diction. Chapter 14 explains, clearly and simply, how to acknowledge the sources you have used.

Writing Essays also includes a case study of one student, Audrey, as she works her way through each component of the process of writing an essay. You will hear from Audrey and follow her along as she considers her topic, does some research, plans her essay, drafts her paragraphs, revises, edits and compiles her source list. By watching over Audrey's shoulder as she methodically works her way through the process of writing her essay, you will gain a solid understanding of what you need to do to write successful essays yourself and an understanding of how to proceed.

Writing Essays will, in short, teach you those skills in written composition that you will call upon to succeed in the many school, college, and university courses that require academic writing.

Derek Soles
derek.soles@studymates.co.uk

1 Getting Started

One-minute overview

If you are like most students, you begin work on an academic essay immediately, by annotating the assignment sheet containing the list of topics your teacher or tutor has given you. You circle the number of the topic that most appeals to you, underline a key phrase or two and make a few preliminary notes about main points to cover and references to check. Perhaps you then put a question mark beside another topic or two that you could turn to if your first choice doesn't work out. Perhaps in other topics you find information which might provide some insights into the topic you have chosen. This is a good strategy, a good place to begin. Having selected your topic, you then must consider the expectations of your tutor, who is, after all, going to be judging your work. What exactly does he or she want from you? Next, you must be clear about the purpose of your academic essay. Why are you writing this essay? What do you want to accomplish? What are your goals? Next, you need to think about your topic, determining especially how much you already know about it and how much more you need to learn. Finally, you need to compose your thesis, the controlling idea of your essay. In other words, to get started writing an academic essay, you need to:

- consider your reader
- establish your purpose
- think about your topic
- compose your thesis statement.

Considering your reader

In the process of researching a subject, synthesising that research, and shaping it into a coherent text, you will learn that subject thoroughly. By writing an essay about a subject, you master it in a way you could not do merely by reading or listening to a lecture. You learn more efficiently and remember longer knowledge you have expressed in written form.

You don't, however, write academic essays only for yourself. You write them to display to your tutors the extent to which you understand an aspect of the content of a course you are taking. Your tutors will read your essay, decide on its worth, and give it a grade. For this reason, it is crucial that, before you begin to write, you consider the expectations of your reader.

Readers influence content

Your primary reader is your teacher. You might share your essay with a classmate, a friend, or a family member and get their input before you hand your essay in. Your tutor might show your essay to a colleague or share it with the rest of the class. But your primary reader is your teacher and it is his or her needs and expectations you must meet. In other words, you must match the **content** of your essay to the needs and expectations of your reader.

Begin by reading the assignment sheet and list of topics with extreme care. Look for terms like 'describe', 'explain', 'define', 'analyse', 'compare and contrast', 'discuss'. These are key clues to your tutor's expectations. If your topic is **describe and explain the process** of photosynthesis, that is exactly what you must do. If your topic is **discuss the causes** of the First World War, do not compare and contrast the peace settlement of the First World War with the peace settlement of the Second World War. If you are asked to **compare and contrast** 'Ode to a Nightingale' and 'Ode on a Grecian Urn', do not **discuss** the life of John Keats, except insofar as it might be relevant to the main topic. The first few words of the topic usually identify the focus your professor expects you to take. Successful writers accommodate their reader's expectations.

Be clear about the required length of your essay, as well. Length will determine the level of detail you are expected to provide. An economics tutor, for example, could ask for a 1,000-word or a 5,000-word essay on the law of supply and demand; the length would dictate the level of detail you would include in such an essay. Meet or exceed slightly the required length. If you do not, your ideas are not likely to be developed in the detail your tutor wants.

Finally, clarify any important aspect of the assignment your teacher may not have made clear. Question anything not clear to you: Do you want us to include a plot summary along with our analysis of the story? How many sources do you expect us to cite? Are there sources you would particularly recommend? How many words do you want? May we use subtitles? The more you know about what your reader wants, the more successful your writing will be.

Readers influence style

Style identifies the manner in which you present information to your readers. If you are sending an email to your friend, your writing style will be informal; your sentence structure might be fragmented; you will probably use slang; you will not be overly concerned about spelling.

The readers of your academic essays, on the other hand, are well-educated women and men working with you in an academic setting. They will expect you to present your information in a fairly mature and relatively formal writing style. You should not be flippant or sarcastic in an academic essay, nor, at the other extreme, should you be pedantic. Try to strike a balance with a style that is smooth and natural but appropriate for a well-educated reader. Most of your textbooks should be written in such a style and might provide you with a model to emulate.

Readers judge quality

Your friend who receives your email will not judge your

sentence structure, paragraph structure, spelling, or grammar. Your tutor who grades your academic essay will.

Try to find out everything you can about the criteria that your tutor will use to assess your work. If your tutor provides you with a list of the criteria, work closely with it as you write and revise your essay. If your tutor does not provide the class with specific information about how essays will be evaluated, try to get some general guidelines at least. Studies clearly indicate that students who understand the criteria on which their writing will be judged write better essays than students who do not know how their teachers will evaluate their writing.

Establishing your purpose

After you have considered the needs of your reader, consider your purpose in writing this academic essay. We write for many reasons: we write a letter to exchange news with friends; we write a poem to express our feelings; we keep a journal to record daily observations.

Academic writing has usually one of two purposes: to provide information which a teacher has requested or to advance an argument about an issue related to the subject you are studying. In other words, academic essays are generally written in either the informative (also known as the expository) rhetorical mode or in the persuasive rhetorical mode.

The informative mode

An informative essay presents complete and accurate information about a specific topic. If you are asked to discuss the causes of the war between Kosovo and Yugoslavia or to explain how to treat a victim of a heart attack or to define post-structuralism or to compare and contrast Freudian and Jungian methods of treating obsessive-compulsive disorder or to explain the rules of cricket, you will write an informative essay. The purpose of an informative essay is to provide your reader with information he or she has requested or can use.

Here is an example of a paragraph written in the informative mode. It is from an essay that explains to readers how to choose an appropriate bottle of wine. Notice that the information provided is specific and detailed, the result mainly of the author's use of examples in support of the paragraph's main idea.

> *The good host will also know something about the grapes from which wines are made, if he is to make just the right choice for his dinner guests. A wine made from the cabernet sauvignon grape will be rich and deep red and will go best with red meats, especially pot roasts, steaks, ribs, and lamb. Wines made from the chardonnay grape, on the other hand, produce dry white wines that will go well with main courses made from fish, shellfish, poultry, and veal. Wines made from the pinot noir grape will also be red, but lighter than those made from the cabernet sauvignon. Pinot noir wines are the perfect complement to barbequed red meat and chicken. The gewürztraminer grape, native to Germany, produces dry white wines with exotic perfumes, which are perfect complements to Asian food – Japanese and Thai dishes especially. With a vegetarian meal, a light and crisp wine made from the sauvignon blanc grape, with its wonderful aroma of grass and pea pods, is ideal.*

A special type of informative writing, known as the **literature review**, is an important part of much academic writing. The 'lit review' is a component of masters theses, doctoral dissertations and research studies; it is the section where authors put their own study in context by reviewing related work done earlier on the subject of their investigation. If, for example, a psychologist were designing and conducting a study to investigate the effect of aging on memory loss, she would need a special section of her report to review relevant past studies. Here is an excerpt from such a lit review:

Gershin (2001) conducted a longitudinal study to measure memory loss among residents of a nursing home in Cornwall. The study was done over a ten-year period with 23 residents who were in their late 70s at the start of the study. Gershin found that there was an average of an 8% memory loss per resident per year over the ten-year period, based upon written and verbal tests that asked residents to recall names of close relatives and famous people. She also found that memory loss escalated as the years passed, so that in the last two years of the ten-year period, the 18 residents still participating were experiencing a 24–30% memory loss. Westin (2003) got similar results from his five-year study of elderly Japanese nursing home residents, as did Hasslebeck (1999), whose ambitious study involved over 100 residents of a large Florida medium-care facility.

The persuasive mode

The purpose of a persuasive essay is, in part, to present information to your reader but, primarily, to convince or persuade your reader that your views on a particular controversial topic are valid and legitimate. If you are asked to discuss the causes of the war in Iraq, you will write an informative essay, but if you are asked how you feel about the UK's involvement in the war, you will write a persuasive essay. Similarly, if you are asked to define post-structuralism, you will write an informative essay, but if you are asked if you believe post-structuralism is a viable method of literary analysis, you will write a persuasive essay.

Here, for example, is a paragraph from an essay in which the author is attempting to argue that angels are real entities who have been known to intervene in human lives. Notice how the author uses direct testimony to support his argument, an essential strategy for so contentious an argument.

> *More compelling proof that angels exist comes from reports of personal encounters some fortunate people have had. In an interview in the July 2003 issue of* Event Magazine, *retired naval officer Arthur Gilbert claimed he had been praying most of the day for his wife Grace, stricken with terminal cancer, when he got up to answer a knock at his door. According to Gilbert's account: 'There stood a very tall, black-skinned, blue-eyed man who identified himself as Michael and who told me that he had been sent by God to cure Grace.' Here Grace continues the story: 'Michael simply moved his right hand towards me, palm outward, but did not touch me. I felt an incredible heat emanating from Michael's hand and I fainted. Then a strong white light, like one of those searchlights, travelled through my body. I knew something supernatural was happening to me.' Grace's amazed doctor told her two days later that there was no longer any sign of cancer in her body and admitted he had witnessed a medical miracle.*

It is important to know your purpose. By clarifying your purpose in writing an academic essay, you must think about your topic, and, in doing so, you will generate ideas which should be useful to you when you begin to write. Moreover, by establishing your purpose, you begin to get some ideas about designing an effective structure for your essay as a whole. Your work will go more smoothly if you know why you are doing it.

Thinking about your topic

By considering the expectations of your reader and by determining your purpose for writing, you start to understand what you need to say in your academic essay and how you should express yourself. You also need to take some time to think about your topic, to determine what you know already about it. You might be surprised. You might know more about your topic than you think you do. You just need a couple of strategies which will help you mine your long-term memory to rediscover information you have learned in the past. There are several methods writers use to generate ideas. Among the most popular are freewriting and questioning.

Freewriting

Freewriting is a form of brainstorming on paper. It is a technique designed to help unblock the creative process by forcing you to write something – anything – about the subject of your assignment. The process is as follows. Using your assignment as a prompt, write non-stop for a limited period of time, usually about ten minutes. You write whatever comes into your mind without worrying about spelling, grammar, or any other aspects of 'correct' writing. No one but you sees your freewriting. After the ten minutes are up, you read your freewriting and extract from it ideas and information that might be useful to you as you write your essay. You can use these ideas as additional prompts and freewrite again and even a third time if you feel the exercise will yield results.

Freewriting is a good pre-writing exercise, but it can be used at any point during the writing process, whenever you get bogged down or blocked.

Questioning

Journalists are taught the W5 strategy as a way of generating ideas for a story they must cover. They are taught, in other words, to inform their readers about the who, what, when, where, and why (i.e. the five Ws) of the event they are covering.

This strategy can be adapted to academic writing as well. When you have selected your topic, make up a list of W5 questions about it. Who will be reading this essay? What does he or she want from me? Who are the important people relevant to the topic? Where did important events related to my topic take place? What do I want to accomplish? When did the events relevant to my topic take place? Why did events transpire as they did? Why is this subject important?

Some of these questions you will be able to answer and parts of those answers, at least, will eventually find their way into your essay. Some questions you will not be able to answer but by asking them you will at least begin to focus your research. Research strategies are covered in detail in the next chapter.

Composing your thesis statement

The end of the beginning of the writing process is the thesis statement. The thesis statement is an expression of the central or controlling idea of your entire essay. It is the essence of your academic essay, what would be left if you put your essay into a pot and boiled it down to its most essential component.

Your thesis might be very specific and incorporate the specific aspects of your topic. Here is an example of such a thesis statement:

> *To take good pictures, a photographer must pay attention to composition, lighting, and point of view.*

Such a thesis is effective because it provides your reader with a blueprint, a mini-plan of the body of your essay. It suggests to the reader that those three points – composition, lighting, and point of view – will be developed in more detail in subsequent paragraphs.

For a more complex essay, however, a detailed thesis might be difficult to compose and hard to understand. For such essays, you might prefer a more general thesis, for example:

Today, the narrator of John Donne's poem 'The Flea' would probably face a charge of sexual harassment.

This thesis has a persuasive edge to it, which means the writer will have to acknowledge and refute opposing points, then develop and support her own argument. Here a general thesis is preferable because a blueprint thesis would have to encompass so much that it would probably be unwieldy.

The thesis statement is often the final sentence of the introductory paragraph. It might be spread over two sentences if the essay is long and complex. Some excellent academic essays do not even contain a recognisable single-sentence thesis in their introductions, but the essay's central idea will certainly be implicit within the essay's introduction. Many tutors, however, do like and expect to see a clear, written thesis within the introduction of an academic essay.

Note, finally, that at this stage of the writing process your thesis statement is preliminary. As you think more about your topic, do some research, and write a few paragraphs, your central focus might change and you might return to the beginning of your essay and alter your thesis.

A case study

Audrey is a second-year university student and she is taking a course on the literature of Elizabethan England. Her professor assigns an essay of up to 2,500 words on any topic relevant to the content of the course. Audrey has always loved Shakespeare's sonnets and was intrigued by one of her professor's lectures, which touched upon the possibility that the characters in the sonnets were real people whom the poet knew. She decides to write her essay on the possible prototypes for the characters in the sonnets.

As we have seen in this chapter, to get started Audrey needs to consider her reader, determine her purpose and try some freewriting, all of which she hopes will lead to at least a preliminary thesis.

She begins by considering her reader:

> *My reader is Professor Fareed, an expert in Elizabethan literature. Obviously she knows Shakespeare's sonnets inside and out. She's not going to need me to explain any of the poems for her. I've got to review the evidence that exists about who these sonnet characters were and present this evidence. She's not going to appreciate any wild theories that amateur Shakespeareans might have developed. I've got to go for the authoritative information. I've got to restrict myself to the genuine experts in the field. Professor Fareed wants an intelligent, scholarly and considered approach to this topic.*

Audrey considers her purpose:

> *My purpose in writing this essay is to explore the possibility that the characters who reoccur in the sonnet sequence were real people Shakespeare knew. At this point, I don't plan to make a case one way or the other: I may argue that the sonnets are autobiographical; I may argue that the characters in them and their actions are fictitious. At this point I don't know if this will be an informative [see page 4] or a persuasive [see page 6] essay. I'll wait and see where my research leads me.*

Audrey does a few minutes of freewriting:

> *I've loved Shakespeare's sonnets ever since I was 14 and we had to read 'When in Disgrace with Fortune and Men's Eyes'. Since then I've read most of them, and this is one of the main reasons why I took Fareed's class. In one of her lectures she speculated on the identities of the 'fictitious' characters who appear*

throughout the sonnets. I knew there has been much literary-historical-biographical speculation about the identities of these characters but I have never really had the time or inclination to investigate further. Now I do. Who exactly is the dark lady? Who is the rival poet? Who is the nobleman to whom the sonnets are dedicated? There's a lot of research I'll have to do. I'll try the Internet then books and journals in the library. How to plan the essay: work my way – and my reader's way – through the sonnets and comment on possible biographical allusions as I go? Isolate each character and have a section in the essay on each? I'll experiment with both. Should I take a stand? Should I try to prove the characters were real or try to prove they were fictitious? I'll probably just consider the possibility that they were real, but I'm getting ahead of myself. Let me do the research first.

Audrey considers a preliminary thesis:

Audrey, wisely, has not yet decided whether she is going to present an argument that the characters in the sonnets have real-life counterparts or merely put forward the evidence and let her readers make up their own minds. She is therefore considering several different possible thesis statements at this early phase in the process:

There is solid evidence to suggest that the rich nobleman, the dark lady and the rival poet were real people and that the sonnets tell of their relationships with Shakespeare.

While the possibility that the rich nobleman, the dark lady and the rival poet had real-life counterparts is intriguing, convincing evidence that Shakespeare's sonnet characters are based upon real people does not exist.

Many scholars, encouraged by Shakespeare's tendency to base his characters on real people, have suggested that, taken together, the sonnets tell a story based on the poet's own experiences and that the characters in the sonnets have real-life prototypes.

Note that by taking the knowledge she already has about the sonnets and by engaging in some 'pre-writing' exercises and activities, Audrey is getting a good start on her project, even though she has not done any hard research yet. By reflecting upon the needs and expectations of her reader, she has a much clearer focus for the content of her essay and the style in which it should be written. By reflecting upon her purpose in writing the essay, she realises she will eventually have to choose between several rhetorical options as she researches and plans her work. By doing some freewriting, she reveals what she already knows about her topic and is already generating some useful content.

Note how, at this stage of the process, Audrey leaves many of her options open. She has a choice of a number of rhetorical modes and thesis statements. Because the goals of a writing assignment can (and often do) change as the writer researches, plans and drafts her work, it is important not to commit completely to any course of action. Strong writers remain flexible and are always open to new information that might change their approach or new ways of expressing a thought or idea.

Tutorial

Progress questions

1. What is the difference between a persuasive and an informative essay?
2. How can you generate ideas for an academic essay?

Discussion points

1. Why is profiling your reader an important and useful pre-writing activity?
2. Why is determining your purpose an important and useful pre-writing activity?
3. What are the benefits of freewriting?

Practical assignment

Select a popular magazine you read on a fairly regular basis. Describe in writing the target audience of this magazine. By examining the articles, the advertisements, and the letters to the editor, you should get a good idea about the type of reader the magazine appeals to.

Study and revision tips

1 Keep the needs and expectations of your reader in mind throughout the writing process, not just before you begin to write.

2 Freewriting can be used at any time during the writing process, especially if you feel you are beginning to suffer from writer's block.

1 Writers often alter or even change completely their thesis statement at different stages of the writing process.

2 Researching Your Topic

One-minute overview

In Chapter 1, you learned how important it is to consider the needs of your reader, determine your purpose, and think about your topic before you begin a draft of your essay. These exercises will help get you started and provide you with some focus. After you have thought about your topic, you must find out as much as you can about what the experts have to say. An academic essay demands research. Research will provide you with much of the information you will need, in order to develop the ideas you present in your essay. Research also lends that aura of authority to your work, which your tutor or teacher will expect. There are basically three sources of information you will need to access in order to research your topic completely. They are:

- books
- periodicals
- the Internet.

Finding the right books

To find book titles which will provide some of the information you will need to discover and develop the ideas you will present in your essay, check your course outline to see if your tutor has included a bibliography or a list of further reading relevant to the course material. If he or she has, and if the list includes a title that sounds as if it is relevant to your topic, do all you can to find the book and see if it contains relevant information. Study also any bibliographies or lists of further or related reading at the end of textbook chapters or at the end of the textbook itself. Most textbooks contain bibliographies and they are invaluable sources of potentially useful information.

Assuming you have found from your course outline or your textbook a list of a dozen or so promising titles, go to your library and check the card catalogue to see if your library has the books and if they are available. Almost all libraries are computerised now, so you must go to a terminal (usually located throughout the library) and follow the instructions (which should be close by) on how to find out if your library has the book you need. The process usually involves typing in the author's name and the title. If your library has the book, the computer screen will tell you where in the library the book is located by providing you with a **call number**. The call number is a series of letters and numbers indicating where, in the library, the book is stored. If, for example, the call number is PE 1471.S65 1997, you find the book shelf with the PE label on it and move down the aisle until you find your number. The screen will also tell you whether or not the book is in or has been signed out, and, if it has been signed out, when it is due back. If it is not due back for a long time, you can usually put a recall on it and get it sooner.

If you have not found any specific titles from course outlines or textbook bibliographies, you will have to do a search by subject. Instead of typing authors' names and book titles into the library computer, try typing in various versions of the subject of your essay. If, for example, you were taking a music history course and had to write an essay on the English madrigal, type in the word 'madrigal' as a subject search and you are bound to get some leads. You can also type in a name as a subject, so for your madrigal essay you could find sources by typing in the names 'Orlando Gibbons', 'Thomas Weelkes', or other English madrigal composers, not as authors' names but as subjects. Begin by making your subject search as specific as possible so that you get the most relevant information. Avoid making your search too broad because you will be overwhelmed by the number of books you can access.

Remember, as well, to check reference books such as encyclopaedias and biographical and other specialised dictionaries. Such books are useful if you need an overview of your topic. The 1997 edition of the *Encyclopaedia Britannica,* for example, has a seven-paragraph history of the madrigal, tracing its origins in fourteenth-century Italy, and describing its popularity in sixteenth-century England.

Finally, you can check theses and dissertations, which are lengthy studies carried out by university students as part of their requirements to obtain an advanced degree. Theses and dissertations are vetted by experts, usually a team of the students' professors, so they are reliable and authoritative, and are often excellent, readable sources for undergraduates working on a writing assignment. To access a thesis or a dissertation, go to *library.dialog.com/bluesheets/html/bl0035.html.*

Checking periodicals

Periodicals are texts published at regular intervals: daily, weekly, monthly, quarterly or yearly. They include newspapers, magazines, and academic journals. Some periodicals are aimed at the general reader; some are aimed at readers interested in a specific topic or academic discipline. There are thousands of them, at least one about any topic you can imagine.

Journals are invaluable sources of information for your academic essays. The advantage they have over books is their currency. Because they are published so regularly, the information in them is usually up to date.

To find a journal article which will provide you with information you might be able to use in an academic essay, you need to access a **periodical index.** Periodical indexes are available in print but the print versions are being superseded by their online siblings.

There should be, on the menu of the computer screen in your college library, a list of the periodical indexes available. The computer in my university library, for example, lists these indexes: applied science and technology, art, general science, humanities, reader's guide, and social sciences. To find information about madrigals, I called up the humanities index and typed the word 'madrigal' on the subject line. On my screen appeared twenty-six titles, including 'Filippo Storzzi and the early madrigals', 'Thomas Morley and the Italian madrigal tradition', and 'Thomas Weelkes' Borrowings from Salamone Rossi'. I called up the last of these and found out that the article was written by Judith Cohen and that it appeared on pages 110 to 117 of the April, 1985, volume 66 issue of the journal *Music and Letters.* I returned then to the main menu, typed in the journal title, and learned that the call number for this journal is ML5.M64.

With the call number, of course, you can find your journal the same way you would find a book in the library stacks. Note that the most recent issues of journals are often kept in a periodicals reading room, not the stacks, and that they are sometimes organised not by call number, but alphabetically.

Searching the Internet

The Internet has become a valuable research tool. There is a warehouse of information stored in cyberspace, and it is relatively easy to access. First you need to log on to the Internet, usually done by clicking the appropriate icon on your computer screen. Next you must select a search engine, which is a database containing a wide variety of information, usually organised by subject. Click onto the search engine, type in the subject, and you will be offered access to a lot of information. A good search engine will help you refine your search so you get exactly what you are looking for.

To find Internet information on the English madrigal composer Thomas Weelkes, for example, I selected the AltaVista search engine and typed in Weelkes' name on the search line. AltaVista offers 325 web pages on Weelkes, some of which are audio, which means you can not only learn something about the composer but also listen to some of his music online.

You must exercise some caution when accessing information from the Internet. Anyone can publish anything on the Internet, including misinformation and disinformation. You must make certain the website you are using is authoritative. If it is affiliated with an institution of higher learning or associated with a known expert in the field you are investigating, the information should be valid. Unless you have a way of authenticating Internet information, be wary of using it.

Consulting your librarian

If you are having trouble finding information about your topic, if you are having trouble using the library computer, if you aren't sure where something is located in the library, don't hesitate to consult your librarian. Librarians are experts at tracking down information, and I have never met one who was unwilling to help.

Our case study continued

Having mulled over the needs and expectations of her reader, considered her aim in writing her essay and spent some time freewriting, Audrey is ready to research her topic: the characters in Shakespeare's sonnets and the possibility they had real-life counterparts.

As almost all students do today, Audrey begins her research by logging on to the Internet and going to her favourite search engine. Into the subject line she types 'characters in

Shakespeare's sonnets' (without quotation marks). The search engine gives her a list of some 11,000 websites. Audrey proceeds to scan the descriptors of the sites and she calls up about a dozen that seem promising. Thereafter, the sites become less and less relevant to her topic. Of the dozen sites she scans, several contain the texts of the sonnets (some with commentary), while others feature bright colours and flashing lights to get her attention and encourage her to buy essays about the sonnets or order books about them. Audrey finds one promising site specifically about the identity of the three characters she is researching, but it is a personal website and the identity of the author is not completely clear. This is a problem because such sites can be unauthoritative and unreliable. Other sites link to this one, though, which suggests the site has some credibility, as does the fact that the author includes a bibliography of authoritative sources. But Audrey will have to use information from this site with discretion. Her Internet search rewards her with a few other promising leads, which she might return to later and pursue. But her plan now is to walk over to her university library and look for books and journal articles about her topic.

At the library, Audrey goes to the computer that catalogues all the books and journals the library contains and tries a keyword search by typing 'Shakespeare and sonnets' (without quotation marks) into the search line. Up comes a list of more than 400 book titles. Clearly she has not been specific enough so she tries again, this time typing 'Shakespeare and sonnets and characters' into the search line. This time only a dozen books are listed. She jots down the call numbers of the most promising titles.

Audrey then accesses a humanities database that catalogues journal articles. She is overwhelmed by the volume of information available. In one journal alone, the *Shakespeare Quarterly*, there are thousands of scholarly papers about the sonnets, some explicating a single line, a single reference, the structure and even the punctuation of single poems. Here she makes a wise decision: she will stick for now to books about the sonnets and only check journal articles later if she feels the books do not provide her with the information she requires. Were she writing a thesis about the prototypes for the characters in the sonnets, she would have to study the scholarly journals. But for a basic undergraduate essay on a topic about which many books have been written, she is safe to limit her research to authoritative websites and books. Some of the books she will eventually select are collections of the best articles that originally appeared in journals, so in a sense she has that base covered anyway.

Audrey goes to the third floor of her library where the books she needs are located and makes her selections. While she is doing this, other potentially useful and relevant titles catch her eye. By the time she has completed her search, she has eleven books relevant to her topic including many by scholars who are recognised experts in the field.

Audrey signs out the eleven books, stuffs as many as she can into her backpack, precariously balances the remaining ones in her arms, catches the bus back to her flat and drops the books onto her desk.

She then begins to read, making notes as she goes. Some student writers use index cards at this point in the process, since using cards forces the researcher to make clear, concise notes. Audrey simply uses a separate notebook. She begins with all of the relevant bibliographical information – full title, author's complete name, place of publication and date of publication. She is careful to put page numbers after the notes she makes. There is nothing more frustrating than returning a borrowed book to the library and then having to go and find it again, after discovering you need it for a page number or an author's first name that you forgot to include during the note-taking phase. Carefully write down all of the information that must appear in your source list at the end of the essay to avoid this inconvenience.

As she works, Audrey is careful to limit her notes to information clearly relevant to her topic and, in so doing, she is beginning to formulate a plan – a structure for her essay.

Tutorial

Progress questions

1. When should you do your research for an academic essay you must write?
2. What is a call number?
3. What is a search engine?

Discussion points

1. What are the advantages and disadvantages of searching for information on the Internet?
2. What advantages do journal articles have over books? Do books have advantages over journal articles?

Practical assignment

1. Find the call number of a book written by one of your tutors.
2. Find the titles of three journals which should contain information relevant to your course of study.
3. Find a website which should contain information relevant to your course of study.

Study and revision tip

Check your textbooks for bibliographies, lists of additional reading, lists of related reading, and references. You can often find titles relevant to your area of interest, and your research will be easier if you have a specific book or journal title to look for.

3 How to Make a Plan

One-minute overview

A plan is a point-form summary of the main ideas and supporting ideas you want to include in your essay. A plan sometimes uses a system of numbers and letters to indicate which points are main ideas and which are supporting ideas. Planning is an important part of the writing process. In this book, planning follows thinking and researching as steps in the writing process, and, indeed, most writers probably do most of their planning at this point. But planning really begins when you annotate your assignment sheet and choose a topic, and it continues while you write and revise your essay. Always remember that planning an academic essay is an ongoing process, not a single step along the road to the production of a text. In this chapter, you will learn about possible ways of planning an essay in the three modes in which academic essays are generally written:

- planning an informative essay
- planning a compare/contrast essay
- planning a persuasive essay.

Planning an informative essay

The key to planning an informative essay lies in the way in which the topic is framed. If you are asked to describe a process, your plan will probably highlight the stages of that process. If you are asked to define a concept, your plan will probably highlight the elements of the definition and/or the examples you plan to use to illustrate the concept. If you are asked to analyse something, a poem, for example, your plan will probably highlight those features (form, theme, metaphor) of the poem you wish to discuss.

Your plan can be detailed or sketchy. You can use a system of numbers and letters to indicate titles and subtitles or simple dashes and indentations. Your plan is made of clay, not granite. You will want to massage it throughout the writing process to change it as you discover new insights into and new information about your topic.

Suppose, for example, you are to write an essay briefly tracing the history of the English language. Such a topic would presuppose a chronological plan:

Title: English – The First One Thousand Years

Thesis: Since its beginnings a thousand years ago, English has evolved and changed under the influence of a variety of social and historical forces.

I. Old English

A. The influence of the Angles and the Saxons
B. The Celtic influence
C. The Vikings
D. Old English Literature

II. Middle English

A. The Norman Conquest
B. Chaucer
C. The printing press

III. Modern English

A. William Shakespeare
B. The King James Version of the Bible
C. The Discovery of the New World

Conclusion: English continues to evolve and change under the influence of technical innovations and a shrinking world.

With a plan such as this, your transition to paragraphing is facilitated because you can concentrate less on where the paragraph will go and more on how it will read, at least in its first draft. Here, for example, are drafts of the paragraphs that would follów from Part I, sections A and B of the above plan:

> *Old English is a Germanic language, born in the wake of the invasion of England by German tribes, most notably the Angles and the Saxons, during the 5th century. 'England', in fact, is a derivation of 'Angleland'. Their language was a branch of Indo-European, which dates back to about 5000 B.C. and from which modern European and even some Asian languages developed.*
>
> *When the Angles and the Saxons landed on English shores, they were met by an even earlier group of Indo-Europeans, the Celts, whom they forced north and west, where today live Celtic descendants, the Welsh, Scots, Irish and Cornish. The Celts were no strangers to invaders, having been victims of Roman imperialism from 55 B.C. to the early part of the fifth century, when the mighty Roman Empire began to collapse. Some English place names, Manchester and Winchester, for example, are derived from the Roman word 'castra,' meaning 'camp'.*
>
> *The Celts fought hard against the German invaders and under King Artorius – probably the legendary King Arthur – had some success. But the Anglo-Saxons were determined to mine the rich minerals and farm the fertile soil of this beautiful island and soon routed the Celts, adding insult to injury by calling them 'wealas', which means foreigners and which is the Anglo-Saxon root word for 'Wales' and 'Welsh'.*

Planning a compare/contrast essay

The compare/contrast essay, in which you are asked to discuss the similarities and differences between two related subjects (two literary works, two economic systems, two political systems, two psychological theories), is commonly assigned in most school, college and university courses. There are two ways of organising a compare/contrast essay: the common traits method or the similarities/differences method.

The common traits method is the best method to use if you are writing primarily an informative essay. If you are writing an essay comparing London and Paris, for example, you might decide to highlight the people, the climate, and the architecture, in which case your plan might look like this:

Comparing and Contrasting London and Paris

Thesis: In various interesting ways, the people, the climate, and architecture of Paris and London are similar to and different from each other.

- I. People
  - A. London
    - reserved
    - polite
    - friendly in pubs
  - B. Paris
    - can seem rude
    - fun-loving
    - pride in personal appearance
- II. Climate
  - A. London
    - rain
    - four seasons
  - B. Paris
    - rain
    - seasons – Paris in the springtime
- III. Architecture
  - A. London
    - royal residences
    - churches and cathedrals
    - government buildings
  - B. Paris
    - museums
    - churches and cathedrals
    - contemporary buildings

Conclusion: Both Paris and London deserve their reputations as first-class residential and tourist cities.

The similarities/differences method is the best one to use if your compare/contrast essay has a persuasive edge to it: that is, if your purpose is to suggest that one of the two items you are comparing and contrasting is superior to the other.

Suppose, for example, you were comparing and contrasting the whole-language method and the phonics method of teaching reading to young children, and you wanted to suggest that the whole-language method was superior. Your plan might look like this:

Two Methods of Teaching Children to Read

Thesis: Educators are divided over how to teach children to read, though the weight of the evidence now favours the whole-language method.

I. Similarities

A. Both methods have the same aim.
B. Both methods are validated by research.
C. Most teachers use both methods, at some point.

II. Differences

A. Children enjoy the whole-language method more.
B. Teachers enjoy teaching the whole-language method more.
C. The whole-language method is more authentic.
D. The whole-language method teaches not only reading but also values and attitudes.

Conclusion: While both methods of teaching reading are effective, the whole-language method offers additional benefits that the phonics method does not.

Planning a persuasive essay

In Chapter 1, you learned that informative and persuasive essays are the two rhetorical modes in which most academic essays are written. The purpose of a persuasive essay is to convince your reader that your opinion on an issue is valid.

Planning a persuasive essay is similar to planning an informative essay. In an informative essay, you present details, facts, anecdotes, and examples to support your main ideas. In a persuasive essay, you present arguments in support of your main ideas – arguments supported by facts, details, and examples.

There is, however, one key difference in planning a persuasive essay. A persuasive essay advances an argument: there are two sides, at least, to an argument; and you must acknowledge and refute the argument that opposes the one you are advancing. To refute means to point out weaknesses in an argument and to present evidence which reveals that argument's limitations. It is important to acknowledge and refute the opposing argument, so you don't appear, to your reader, to be shying away from anything that might weaken your case.

You should build into your plan a section wherein you will summarise and refute the position contrary to your own. It does not really matter where in the essay the refutation appears. For some of the argumentative essays you write, you will want to address and refute the opposition early; for others, your case might be stronger if you delay the refutation until the end.

Shown opposite is a plan for a persuasive essay, the thesis of which is that the plays attributed to William Shakespeare were actually written by Edward de Vere, 17th Earl of Oxford.

Conclusion

Planning is an important part of writing a sound academic essay. Do not, however, get locked into a formal, carefully structured plan early in your process of writing your essay. A plan should be fluid and flexible. You should design a careful, formal plan for your essay. But allow your plan to change as you write your essay. Writing is, among many things, a process of discovery and you might discover a more effective way of organising and presenting your thoughts and ideas as you work through successive drafts of your essay. You might have a fresh insight or discover a good research source which contains information which will strengthen your paper. Be willing to alter your plan as you work. If your tutor wants you to hand in a plan or outline of your essay with the essay itself, compose that final version of your outline later rather than earlier in the process.

Alias William Shakespeare: The Case for the de Vere Authorship

Thesis: Overwhelming evidence exists indicating that Edward de Vere is the real author of the great plays and poems attributed to William Shakespeare.

- A. The author had a classical education and an insider's knowledge of the court.
    1. Shakespeare's background and education.
    2. de Vere's background and education.
- B. Oxford (de Vere) artefacts.
    1. The Oxford Bible contains annotated and underlined passages found in the plays.
    2. The Oxford coat of arms depicts an English lion shaking a broken spear.
- C. Characters in the plays.
    1. Hamlet, Falstaff, Lear, and Prospero have experiences strikingly similar to some of Oxford's own.
    2. Polonious as Lord Burghley.
    3. Helena as Anne Cecil.
- D. The sonnets
    1. The story the sonnets tell mirrors Oxford's own life.
    2. The characters in the sonnets resemble people he knew.
- E. Refute opposition
    1. Oxford hid his authorship because it was unseemly for aristocrats to be too involved in the theatre.
    2. The dating of the plays is uncertain so the fact that Oxford died in 1604 does not prove he did not write plays allegedly written after his death.

Conclusion: The case for Oxford is strong and will grow stronger as more about Oxford's life is discovered.

Our case study continued

Having considered her TAP (topic, audience, purpose) and researched her topic, Audrey is ready to proceed to the next phase of writing an academic essay – considering and developing a plan and formulating a structure. Since writing is a recursive process, she may do additional research later and she will always keep her reader in mind as she plans, drafts and revises. But her focus for now is on developing an outline for her essay.

Purpose influences structure. A compare/contrast essay has a different structure to an argument essay, which has a different structure to a simple informative essay. Audrey considered the possibility of writing an argument, either in support of or in opposition to the notion that the sonnets are based on real people whom Shakespeare knew. But after researching her topic, she has decided to write an informative essay, which suggests but does not insist that the sonnet characters have real-life counterparts.

Her organisational structure, therefore, will be relatively straightforward. She has two choices. She can work her way through the 154 sonnets, commenting on the characters as she goes. Or she can arrange the essay by character, discussing first the close friend, then the dark lady, and finally the rival poet. She selects the latter (though, as we will see when she is in the revision stage of the process, she will modify this plan slightly) because the former would require a longer essay than the one she has been assigned and would result in a less compelling final product.

Audrey shuffles, organises and edits her notes and jottings and finally produces this outline:

Title: Prototypes for the Characters in Shakespeare's Sonnets

Thesis: The people who appear in Shakespeare's famous sequence of 154 sonnets are rendered so authentic that many scholars have suggested that the sonnets tell a story based on the poet's own experiences and that the characters in the sonnets have real-life prototypes.

A. The patron/friend

1. Henry Wriothesley – age right; initials wrong; appearance and social status right
2. William Herbert – initials right; age wrong; appearance and social status right
3. William Harvey – appearance and social status wrong; family connection; circumstantial evi dence.

B. The dark lady

1. Elizabeth Vernon – her relationship with Wriothesley
2. Mary Fitton – her relationship with Herbert
3. Emilia Lanier – Rowse's choice based again on circumstantial evidence; tenuous connection to Shakespeare and Wriothelsley.

C. The rival poet

1. Samuel Daniel – wrote a sonnet sequence; right style
2. George Chapman – wrote a sonnet sequence; right style
3. Christopher Marlowe – as well-known as Shakespeare; gay; early death supports sonnet chronology.

Conclusion: The possibility that the characters are real is intriguing and there is compelling evidence to suggest they are, though this evidence is circumstantial.

Tutorial

Progress questions

1. When should you design a plan for an academic essay?
2. What are the two methods of planning a compare/contrast essay? Is one method more effective than the other? Explain your answer.

Discussion points

1. Why is it important to develop a plan before beginning to write an essay?
2. Why is it important to acknowledge and refute the opposition in a persuasive essay?

Practical assignment

Carefully read a chapter in one of your textbooks and compose the plan the author might have worked with as he or she composed that chapter.

Study and revision tip

Remember that planning is an ongoing process. You can tinker with your plan as you write and revise your essay.

4 Analysing and Interpreting Information

One-minute overview

In the previous chapter, we learned how to plan informative, compare/contrast, and persuasive essays. We focused on these genres because they are common forms of academic writing. Another common academic assignment is the subject of this chapter: writing the essay of analysis and interpretation. Students in philosophy, economics, business, history, literature, psychology, sociology, anthropology, women's studies, cultural studies, and political science courses are frequently required to write essays of analysis and interpretation. Analyse and interpret Book I of *Paradise Lost*, the foreign policy of Clement Attlee, Van Gogh's *Starry Night*, the anti-inflation policies of Margaret Thatcher, Henry VII's role in discrediting Richard III, the advertising campaign of the Jaguar S-Type automobile: if you have been a college student for more than two years you have undoubtedly encountered assignments similar to these. Analysis is the process of dividing your subject of study, your topic, into its component parts. Interpretation is the process of assessing and describing how those parts coalesce into a coherent whole and cause the enterprise you are analysing to succeed or to break down. To write a successful analysis/interpretation essay, then, you must:

- define the distinguishing features of the whole
- divide the whole into its component parts
- analyse the parts
- interpret the relationship of the parts to the whole.

Defining the distinguishing features of the whole

Suppose your assignment is to write an analysis and interpretation of Shakespeare's 33rd sonnet, 'Full Many a Glorious Morning Have I Seen'. You would begin such an analysis by defining the features of the whole:

> *A Shakespearean sonnet is a brief poem containing fourteen lines, each of which is composed of five iambic beats. The sonnet is divided into three four-line stanzas or quatrains of alternating rhyme. It ends with a rhyming couplet, which forms lines thirteen and fourteen. The rhyming couplet is usually epigrammatic and neatly and concisely presents the poem's main theme. Among Shakespeare's most famous and most beautiful sonnets is 'Full Many a Glorious Morning Have I Seen'.*

Dividing the whole into its component parts and analysing the parts

You would proceed by dividing the whole into its component parts, and by analysing each part:

> *The first quatrain is descriptive:*
>
> *Full many a glorious morning have I seen*
> *Flatter the mountain tops with sovereign eye,*
> *Kissing with golden face the meadows green,*
> *Gilding pale streams with heavenly alchemy;*
>
> *The poet describes a beautiful clear summer day. Indeed the imagery he uses to describe this day is Edenic. Adjectives like 'glorious' and 'heavenly', 'sovereign' and 'golden' convey an almost Utopian ambience. The image of the sun kissing the*

meadows and gilding the streams with gold ('heavenly alchemy') heightens this sense of nature's perfections. Clearly, this is going to be a great day.

Or is it? In the second quatrain a cloud appears, and it blocks out the sun:

Anon permit the basest clouds to ride
With ugly rack on his celestial face,
And from the forlorn world his visage hide,
Stealing unseen to west with this disgrace.

A 'rack' is an accumulation of clouds which hides the sun's celestial visage (face) for the rest of the day, until it sets, in disgrace, in the west.

In the third quatrain, the poet draws a unique and striking parallel between the now-shaded sun of heaven and the sunshine of his own life, his best friend. The sun of his best friend seemed to shine only for the poet, 'With all triumphant splendour' (line 10). But, alas, the friend soon turned his attention to another; 'he was but one hour mine,' (line 11) and now the friend is gone.

In the couplet, lines 13 and 14, there is another surprise. We might expect the poet to be bitter and jealous that his friend proved so fickle. But he is not:

Yet him for this my love no whit disdaineth;
Suns of the world may stain when heaven's sun staineth.

If the sun of heaven can turn its attention away from the earth, how can we expect a human sun to remain constant? The poet still loves his friend as much as ever.

Interpreting the relationship of the parts to the whole

The final step in your analysis and interpretation is to evaluate or re-evaluate the whole based upon your analysis and interpretation of its parts. This step, obviously, is crucial. You are judging the success or the failure, the strength or the weakness of the subject of your analysis and interpretation. You are going to say either that the whole is sound because the component parts work in harmony toward a greater purpose or that the whole is unsound because one or some of its parts inhibit a unity of purpose. In the case of our example, our analysis of Shakespeare's 33rd sonnet, the former is the case.

> *Shakespeare cleverly uses a familiar metaphor – you are the sunshine of my life – to present an unexpected theme: love presupposes a willingness to forgive and forget a dear friend's inconstancy. We might admire the poet for his unshakeable devotion; we might condemn him for too easily forgiving a fickle friend, and suspect a weakness in character. Certainly, we admire how Shakespeare imposes the discipline of a sonnet onto the images and metaphors he has assembled, how his words and lines coalesce seamlessly into a unified whole. Like all great works of art, 'Full Many a Glorious Morning Have I Seen' is greater than the sum of its parts.*

Learning how to analyse and interpret

The ability to analyse and interpret – in writing – a text, a government or political policy, a work of art, a mathematical formula, a marketing strategy, a philosophical treatise, a social science theory, a physics principle (the list is as long as the number of courses offered at a comprehensive university) is crucial to your success as a student. We used, as an example here, an analysis and interpretation of a Shakespeare sonnet, but remember that the analytic and interpretive principles we brought to bear can be modified and used in the analyses and interpretations you will have to do for other academic disciplines.

Suppose, for example, you had to analyse, for a business administration class, the efficacy of the marketing plan a company has developed for a certain product. Your analysis would include the same, three-part strategy. First, consider the features of the whole: does the plan clearly and accurately present the company's strategies for selling the most product to the most people for the best price? Second, consider the specific parts of the plan: does the plan discuss what needs the product will fulfill? Does it explain how the company will determine what segment of the population would be most interested in the product? Does it describe how they will use TV, magazines and the various other advertising vehicles to reach these people? Does it identify the competition and how to 'scoop' them? Third, consider the extent to which the parts coalesce to form a harmonious whole. If it is a successful business plan, it will confirm that consumer X needs the product, is willing to pay for it, cannot buy a better version for a better price from another company, reads the magazines and watches the programmes where the product is likely to be advertised and can access the retail outlet where the product will be sold.

Clearly the ability to analyse and interpret is essential to academic success, since it is required in so many academic disciplines. Fortunately, the guidelines presented here can be adapted to fit analytical and interpretive writing assignments in virtually any subject area.

Tutorial

Progress questions

1. What is the difference between the processes of analysis and interpretation?
2. What are the components of a successful analysis?
3. What are the components of a successful interpretation?

Discussion points

1. Discuss each component of an analysis and interpretation essay. Assess the importance of each component in relation to the others.
2. What is meant by the statement: 'The whole is greater than the sum of its parts'?

Practical assignments

1. Compose three assignments related to the discipline you are studying at university, which would require the use of the principles of analysis and interpretation described in this chapter.

---

2. For about ten minutes, observe the behaviour of a friend, a child, one of your teachers, or of anyone you might come in contact with. Try to analyse and interpret that behaviour, using the methods described in this chapter.

Study and revision tips

1. To help you study for a test, you might try to apply the principles of analysis and interpretation discussed in this chapter to the material you are studying.

---

2. Definitions are an important part of analysis and interpretation. Make sure you have defined key terms accurately and clearly.

5 Writing a Clear and Specific Opening

One-minute overview

First impressions are important in academic writing. You want to write an introductory paragraph (or paragraphs, if your assignment is a major research paper), which will engage your readers' interest and encourage them to read on, not because they have to but because they want to. You must also clearly establish the topic of your paper in your opening paragraph or paragraphs, so that the context of your thesis is clear. Finally, you must present that thesis, which will usually appear at the end of your introductory paragraph. In this chapter, we will examine five examples of introductions to academic essays. We will judge, discuss, and analyse the effectiveness of these paragraphs based on the three criteria mentioned above:

- does it engage the reader's interest?
- does it clearly establish the topic?
- does it present the thesis?

Sample introductory paragraph 1

College and university students are often apprehensive about writing essays. The list of the characteristics of good writing seems formidable and intimidating. Tutors want written work to be informative, well-organised, clear, and concise. They want correct grammar, spelling, and punctuation. They want to read essays that have unity and coherence, and some variety in diction and sentence structure. They look for originality and creativity, style and substance. How much there is to keep in mind, students lament, in order to write well. Can't the rules for good writing be made less daunting, more accessible?

> Fortunately, they can. All of the characteristics of good writing can be synthesised and reduced to four fundamental rules. To write well, students must explore their topic, develop their ideas, express themselves clearly, and cultivate an effective style.

Analysis

This paragraph would engage the interest of readers who want to know how to write a good essay, though it has little to grab the attention of a reader not interested in the topic. The question (sentence 8) might motivate reluctant readers to give the essay a try. The context of the paper – overcoming writing apprehension by knowing what tutors look for – is clearly established. The thesis is clearly stated as the paragraph's last sentence. It is a blueprint thesis clearly stating the four points which will be developed in the body of the essay.

Sample introductory paragraph 2

> At the time he wrote 'Ode to a Nightingale', in the spring of 1819, Keats had been diagnosed with tuberculosis, and knew he had not long to live. This news came soon after Keats, who had trained as a physician, had cared for his brother Tom, as he died slowly and painfully of the same fatal illness. In 'Ode to a Nightingale', Keats gives voice to his despair. In the poem, he describes his anguish and his suffering; he expresses his desire to escape from his world of pain and sorrow with the help of the nightingale's beautiful song; and he describes the initial success but ultimate failure of his attempt to escape his reality.

Analysis

This paragraph begins with an anecdote, a story, which is an effective way to engage readers' interest. It clearly indicates that the essay will be about Keats's poem, 'Ode to a Nightingale'. The paragraph ends with a blueprint thesis. The thesis is complex; it is a long sentence, about fifty words. The writer might have gone with a general thesis: 'In

"Ode to a Nightingale", Keats explains how he might try to cope with the despair with which life has surrounded him.' A general thesis, however, might make the introductory paragraph seem rather short.

Sample introductory paragraph 3

> No composer influenced Mozart's work more than the music of Johan Sebastian Bach. Around 1782, living in Vienna, Mozart, then 25, first heard Bach's music. Immediately he began to blend Bach's style and technique with his own. The result was the birth of a new musical style which has come to be known as Viennese Classical.

Analysis

As introductory paragraphs go, this one is a little thin. It is a potentially fascinating topic but the writer has not done as much as she could to convince the reader this subject is interesting enough to pursue in this essay. The writer has established the context for the essay, but the thesis is vague. Will she now describe the nature of the influence in detail or tell her readers about the Viennese Classical style or some combination of both? The writer has not provided her readers with the clear direction they require.

Sample introductory paragraph 4

> The stars in our sky, revealing themselves to us on a clear dark night, appear randomly scattered. There are large gaps where few stars appear and occasional clusters of many stars grouped together. It is as if some divine presence has filled his two hands with many-pointed sparkling rocks and thrown them into the night sky where they have stuck. In fact, astronomers, some of whom worked 5000 years ago, have imposed a pattern on our random collection of stars. At first the patterns were based on a form of celestial connect-the-dots, as ancient astronomers drew imaginary lines connecting stars together and concluded that they resembled

mythological figures: Leo, Taurus, Orion, and so forth. These astronomers lived in the northern hemisphere so they could not map the stars in the southern sky. They missed, as well, distant stars, glowing faintly, even those in their own hemisphere. Then in 1928, the International Astronomical Union established a more sophisticated system, dividing the sky into 88 regions with clearly defined, though invisible, boundaries, much like the boundaries that exist between countries. These 88 celestial countries are called constellations.

Analysis

This introductory paragraph captures the reader's interest in its first few sentences which are well written and interesting, especially the third sentence with its use of metaphor. But soon the paragraph begins to drift and introduces information (about stars in the southern hemisphere and distant stars) which might be better placed within the body of the essay. This is a common flaw among student introductory paragraphs: sometimes they contain information which really belongs later in the essay. Moreover, the paragraph does not exactly contain a thesis. It almost seems complete in itself. The last sentence suggests that the rest of the essay will elaborate on the definition and description of constellations but this is really a guess on the reader's part. An essay's introduction needs to be clear and explicit. After readers have read the introduction, they should know what is coming next.

Sample introductory paragraph 5

For centuries, two hundred to be exact, the life of Jesus has been shrouded in mystery. Only one main source documents his birth, though it does so in the most vivid detail. This source skips his childhood and picks up his story only in the last few of the approximately thirty years he lived. It documents his death with the same intensity with which it documents his birth. This source is, of course, the New Testament. The New Testament is gospel (literally) to some, but most biblical historians read, or have read it

> sceptically, questioning its historical accuracy. In the last forty years, however, new archaeological discoveries have shed new light on Jesus' life. These new discoveries have, for the most part, confirmed, sometimes dramatically, the New Testament account of the life of Christ. Three discoveries in particular suggest that the New Testament authors were much more historians than novelists.

Analysis

This is a good introductory paragraph for an undergraduate academic essay. It engages the reader's interest by virtue of the topic and the clear way in which the topic is presented. It establishes the necessary historical context for the topic. It presents a clear thesis in the last sentence. Readers know what is going to follow.

Our case study continued

Audrey has researched the possible biographical implications of Shakespeare's sonnets and has developed a preliminary outline to guide her as she drafts her paragraphs. She may do some more research and she may refine her outline as she proceeds, but at this point, she is ready to draft some paragraphs.

She wants her opening paragraph to engage the reader, introduce her topic and present her essay's main idea. Here is the first draft of her opening paragraph:

> *The characters in Shakespeare's famous sequence of 154 sonnets are described so authentically that many scholars, encouraged by Shakespeare's tendency to base his characters on real people, have suggested that, taken together, the sonnets tell a story. The story they tell is based on the poet's own experiences and, as a result, the characters in the sonnets have real-life prototypes. These characters are a dear friend of the poet's, a rival poet and a mysterious and beautiful dark lady.*

Audrey knows that this first draft of her opening paragraph will need some work, some revising and some editing. Although it introduces her topic and presents her thesis, it is lacklustre and does not really engage the reader's interest. But it's a good start and she will revise and edit it later, once she has a complete rough draft.

Tutorial

Progress questions

1. Why is it important to try to capture your reader's interest in your opening paragraph?
2. What is a thesis?
3. Why is it important to present your thesis in your opening paragraph?

Discussion points

1. Find in an academic journal or a collection of academic essays related to your course or to a subject you are interested in, an example of an effective opening. Discuss with your Studymates the reasons why you think this opening is effective.
2. Find in an academic journal or a collection of academic essays related to your course or to a subject you are interested in, an example of an ineffective opening. Discuss with your Studymates the reasons why you think this opening is ineffective.

Practical assignment

In an essay of approximately 500 words or in your journal describe the qualities of an opening paragraph which would arouse your interest and encourage you to read the rest of the essay. Provide three examples of such paragraphs.

Study and revision tip

Review the opening paragraph of an academic essay you have already written, turned in, and have had graded and returned to you. Write a one-paragraph evaluation of the quality of your opening based upon the criteria and the examples discussed in this chapter.

6 Writing Complete Body Paragraphs

One-minute overview

Following your introduction, your academic essay will have any number of body paragraphs (depending on the nature of the assignment and the number of words your tutor expects), which will elucidate your thesis. Your body paragraphs will need:

- a topic sentence
- a sufficient number of sentences to elucidate the topic sentence
- unity.

Composing a topic sentence

A body paragraph needs a topic sentence. The topic sentence presents the subject of the paragraph, and the other sentences in the paragraph illuminate the topic sentence. It is to the paragraph what the thesis is to the essay as a whole.

Where in the body paragraph should the topic sentence be? It is often the first sentence. If the first sentence is transitional, that is if it refers back to the content of the previous paragraph, the topic sentence might be the second one. But it can be anywhere. It can work well at the end of the paragraph if the supporting sentences build up to the topic sentence. In this case, the topic sentence becomes the climax of the paragraph. The topic sentence can even, like a thesis statement, be implied from its supporting sentences, but most teachers prefer the clarity which an explicit topic sentence provides to its paragraph.

Developing your topic sentence

A typical paragraph in the body of an academic essay must be developed in enough detail to satisfy the needs and expectations of its readers. In a long essay, you might have a short paragraph to signal a transition from one main idea to the next, or you might write a short body paragraph in the interests of a rhetorical effect such as emphasis. But most paragraphs in the body of an academic essay will consist of at least four sentences, the topic sentence and at least three others in support of the topic. One of the most common faults in undergraduate academic essays is an inadequately developed topic sentence, which creates an underdeveloped paragraph. Make certain your body paragraphs are well developed. Provide details and examples which support and illuminate your topic sentence. Define key words your reader might not be completely familiar with. Use comparisons and contrasts, present causes, describe effects. Relate an anecdote to elucidate your topic sentence, if the anecdote is relevant and useful. Do not leave your body paragraphs underdeveloped.

Maintaining paragraph unity

Body paragraphs must have unity, which means that all of the sentences within the paragraph must develop, explain, add detail to, or otherwise relate to and elucidate the topic sentence. A body paragraph is typically about one subject specified within the topic sentence. All of the other sentences within a body paragraph must relate to the topic sentence. When you are revising your essay, check to make sure all of the sentences in your body paragraphs do relate to the topic sentence. You violate the important principle of paragraph unity if you have sentences in a body paragraph that drift away from the topic. Often these are good sentences which do not relate to the paragraph's topic but do somehow relate to the essay's thesis, and which can, therefore, be used effectively in a different body paragraph. Edit out sentences that destroy paragraph unity or, if possible, integrate them into other paragraphs within which they are relevant.

Sample body paragraphs

Here are five examples of body paragraphs followed by an analysis of their strengths and their weaknesses.

Sample body paragraph 1

> But, today, intelligence and integrity are not enough. We also expect our politicians, in this age of multimedia, to be charismatic. The word 'charisma' is from the Greek word meaning 'gift of grace', and, as the 'grace' aspect of the definition suggests, the word originally had religious connotations. It maintains some of these connotations, as evident in 'charismatic' evangelical sects, who view Christ as the personification of charisma. But its meaning has softened over the years. We do not expect our presidents and prime ministers to be godly, but we do want them to exude a self-confidence and a serenity which, in turn, calms us, the people our politicians will govern. We expect them to light up a room when they enter it, to command the attention of others by virtue of their physical presence alone. Some insist that Bill Clinton has this presence. Mikhail Gorbachev, John F. Kennedy, Pierre Trudeau, certainly Cleopatra, and Nelson Mandela were charismatic political leaders. And Sir Winston Churchill remains, to many, the poster boy for the club of charismatic political leader.

Analysis

This body paragraph has a topic sentence (the second): 'We also expect our politicians, in this age of multimedia, to be charismatic'. The first sentence is transitional, referring back to other traits (discussed in earlier body paragraphs) of good politicians. The topic sentence is well developed through the use of the definition and through examples. Seven sentences develop the topic sentence. The paragraph contains 177 words. All of the sentences relate to the topic sentence, so the paragraph has unity.

Sample body paragraph 2

Even more baffling is the support for the death penalty voiced by members of the Christian right. Christians follow the teaching and emulate the actions of Jesus. One of the most famous New Testament stories reveals Jesus as an abolitionist. A group brought before Jesus a woman who was convicted of adultery, then a capital crime in the Holy Land. Before they stoned the woman to death, they sought advice from their spiritual leader. As John tells the story (8:3–11), Jesus 'lifted himself up and said unto them, "he that is without sin among you, let him cast the first stone" '. The woman was freed, with Jesus' stern admonition that she 'sin no more'. As the personification of the compassion and forgiveness which define Christianity, Jesus opposed the death penalty, as must any who profess to follow the Christian faith.

Analysis

This paragraph is from a persuasive essay in opposition to capital punishment. Its topic 'sentence' is that one argument against the death penalty is that it is anti-Christian. It is not stated as such in so many words but is implicitly clear. It is a good example of the use of an anecdote or story to develop a topic sentence. Perhaps the context story could have been established more clearly. At 142 words, the paragraph has just a bit of room for further development.

Sample body paragraph 3

The real level of social responsibility that corporations need to exercise lies somewhere between the ravings of the Marxists for state control and the 'greed-is-good' mentality of the extreme free marketers. Certainly, multinational corporations set up shop in Third World countries where they can pay workers a fraction of what they would have to pay English workers and thereby increase their treasured profit margin. Yet the governments of these countries are reluctant to nationalise such companies partly because a poor wage by Western standards is often a fair wage by other standards and partly because the governments know they lack the expertise to manage the companies effectively. Comparatively low wages and the spectre of the presence of western capitalism on their sovereign soil is preferable to absolute poverty and the threat of political revolution. On the other hand, there are Western companies that employ children who should be going to school and whom the companies do pay poorly, even by the standards of the countries where they work. Child labour is unconscionable, anathema to developed countries for the past one hundred years. Recently, certain celebrities have been publicly scolded and ridiculed for advertising and even allowing their own name to be placed on clothing made by children who live barely above the poverty level. There are other products besides clothing which Western businesses manufacture in Third World countries to take advantage of low wages. Nor is there any excuse for sub-standard working conditions. Adequate pay will not buy loyalty if Third World workers are subject to lead poisoning, work in factories without sufficient sanitation, and long hours without breaks.

Analysis

Here we have two, maybe three body paragraphs crammed into one. The paragraph touches on Marxism, capitalism, nationalism, child labour, working conditions. The first sentence sounds like a topic sentence for a compare/contrast paragraph but with sentences about celebrities and about other manufactured products, the writer abandons her topic sentence. The paragraph lacks unity. It needs to be divided into two or three paragraphs, each with its own topic sentence well developed. If the writer chooses to write just one paragraph, she needs to edit out the material that doesn't fit.

Sample body paragraph 4

Why does Norma Jean decide to leave Leroy? She decides to leave partly because Leroy annoys her. She admits she was happier when he was driving his truck and was away from home much of the time. Because of his injury, he is always at home now, underfoot, smoking marijuana, and dreaming of building a log cabin, in which Norma Jean has little interest. But the real cause of her discontent, the real reason she leaves, has to do with her new-found identity. Norma Jean has grown up. She is a different person from the eighteen-year-old girl who had to get married because she was pregnant. She is working out, attending college classes, and even thinking about standing up, at last, to her overbearing mother. Leroy, annoyed, asks his wife if all of

> this is some 'women's lib thing'. His retort is meant to be sarcastic, but it contains more truth than he realises or cares to admit.

Analysis

This is a paragraph from a student's essay on Bobbie Ann Mason's story, 'Shiloh'. It is a good example of a body paragraph which uses a question as its topic sentence and then uses the other sentences to answer the question. It is also an example of how a body paragraph can build up to a key point. Minor answers to the topic sentence question are presented early in the paragraph, then the middle sentence begins: 'But the real cause...'. This is an effective way of highlighting the key information that a body paragraph contains. This paragraph is 158 words in length.

Sample body paragraph 5

> A typical paragraph in the body of an academic essay must be developed in enough detail to satisfy the needs and expectations of its readers. In a long essay, you might have a short paragraph to signal a transition from one main idea to the next, or you might write a short body paragraph in the interests of a rhetorical effect such as emphasis. But most paragraphs in the body of an academic essay will consist of at least four sentences – the topic sentence and at least three others in support of the topic. One of the most common faults in undergraduate academic essays is an inadequately developed topic sentence, which creates an underdeveloped paragraph. Make certain your body paragraphs are well developed. Provide details and examples which support and illuminate your topic sentence. Define key words your reader might not be completely familiar with. Use comparisons and contrasts, present causes, describe effects. Relate an anecdote to elucidate your topic sentence, if the anecdote is relevant and useful. Do not leave your body paragraphs underdeveloped.

Analysis

This paragraph contains a clear topic sentence, the first. The second sentence qualifies the topic sentence, indicating that occasionally, a body paragraph might be quite short. The inclusion of such a sentence is common in body paragraphs.

The other eight sentences develop the topic sentence, providing supporting details and explanations. The fifth sentence is somewhat redundant, in that it does little more than rephrase the topic sentence. If it were eliminated the paragraph would still contain 167 words and would still be well developed.

Our case study continued

Audrey has written a draft of her opening paragraph. She now proceeds to draft the body of her essay, keeping in mind the necessary qualities of substance, unity and coherence. Here are four paragraphs from the draft of the body of Audrey's essay:

The patron/friend is featured in sonnets 1–126, the bulk of Shakespeare's collection. The poet describes him as a handsome, indeed beautiful young man, extremely intelligent and refined. This description fits Henry Wriothesley, the Earl of Southampton, and many Shakespeare scholars believe Southampton is the friend featured in many of the sonnets. Southampton was 20 in 1593, when Shakespeare was most likely working on his sonnets (Hubler 12). He was a nobleman and a patron of the arts. Shakespeare explicitly dedicates some of his other poems to Southampton, in a way that suggests they were close friends (Hubler 12). But there is a problem with confirming the identity of Henry Wriothesley as the sonnets' protagonist. The sonnets are dedicated to their 'ONLIE BEGETTER,' whom most experts believe to be the person who inspired the sonnets, in other words the special friend. In the dedication, this friend is identified by his initials. The initials are 'W.H.', which reverses those of Henry Wriothesley. Either the printer made a mistake, the author was being deliberately coy and partially hiding his benefactor's identity, or the Earl of Southampton was not the special friend of the sonnets.

In Sonnet 127, a new character appears on the scene. She is a beautiful, dark-haired woman who becomes the narrator's mistress. But she is unfaithful to the narrator and her infidelity torments him. He suspects that one of her lovers is the patron/friend, and the tone of those sonnets in which he speculates about the double deception reflect the torment of a man unable to deal with the possibility that his two closest friends are deceiving him.

If Wriothesley is the patron/friend, then Elizabeth Vernon is probably the infamous dark lady (Hubler 17). Vernon was a lady-in-waiting to Queen Elizabeth I. As an earl, Wriothesley was regularly at court and, although the Queen expected him to marry another and actually imprisoned him because of his liaison with Vernon, the two nevertheless married in May of 1598. The sonnets were written five years before this, so if Shakespeare and Southampton were indeed competing for the affections of Vernon, Southampton won. The Wriothesleys had a daughter four months after they married (Hubler 17).

The rival poet who makes Shakespeare jealous because he also receives patronage from W.H. is difficult to identify because there were so many poets in Elizabethan England, and most of them sought the patronage of a nobleman. Shakespeare describes his rival's poetic style in ways that suggest, to most experts, the work of Samuel Daniel or George Chapman, both of whom wrote sonnet collections (Hubler 18–19). Dover Wilson makes a strong case for Chapman by explicating sonnet 86 and seeing within it echoes of Chapman's own work, which Shakespeare mocks (lxix). Rowse's choice is the second best poet of the age, Christopher Marlowe. Marlowe was openly gay, and Wriothesley was probably bisexual. Rowse's implication is that there was a sexual empathy, if not a relationship, between the two, that the heterosexual Shakespeare could not handle. There has been much speculation about Shakespeare's sexuality, as revealed in the sonnets, but he does indicate in Sonnet 20 that his own relationship with this friend is non-sexual. The rival poet disappears from the sonnets at about the halfway point in a way that suggests, if the order of the sonnets is chronological, that Shakespeare won the battle for the patron's generosity and that confirms Rowse's belief that Marlowe is the rival. Rowse suggests that Shakespeare's victory was due not to his superior ability but to tragic circumstance. Marlowe was killed in a bar-room brawl in 1593, the time most experts believe Shakespeare was working on his sonnet collection (Rowse xviii). After Marlowe's death, Shakespeare had no rival; hence, the rival poet disappears as a character.

These paragraphs are in draft, remember, so they still need to be revised and edited. But Audrey appears to be on the right track. The first, for example, is 194 words long; not an absolute guarantee of sound development, since there could be redundancy, but one indication that she is developing her ideas well. The fourth paragraph is, at 267 words, also well developed; indeed this is rather long, even for an academic essay, and when she revises Audrey might consider dividing this paragraph into two.

Audrey explicates parts of some of the sonnets, and uses interesting, carefully researched historical details to develop her paragraphs. She carefully cites her sources in parentheses after she has taken a direct quote or used an idea from one of them. (The complete bibliographical information will appear in her source list, at the end of her essay.)

Tutorial

Progress question

Correct the violations in paragraph unity contained within the following passage. You may divide the passage into two paragraphs if you wish. You may add to, but not delete from, the information contained within the passage.

The Castle of Otranto, by Horace Walpole, is another example of a novel of the 'mystery and terror school'. *The Castle of Otranto* is a Gothic novel. Horace Walpole was born in 1717 and died in 1797. He was a novelist and also something of an art critic and historian. A renaissance man, Walpole was a member of the British Parliament from 1741 to 1767. He followed in his father's footsteps. His father, Robert, was twice prime minister of Great Britain. The main character is Manfred, the Prince of Otranto, who decides to marry Isabella, the daughter of the Marquis of Vincenza, after Otranto's son, who was betrothed to Isabella, dies under mysterious circumstances. Isabella wants no part of Manfred and runs off, her escape aided by the Peasant Theodore. A series of supernatural events follows, culminating in the collapse of the castle. Theodore is declared heir and marries Isabella. The Gothic novel is characterised by horror, terror, the supernatural, murder, and violence. Gothic novels are often set in gloomy, isolated castles. Horace Walpole even built his own imitation Gothic castle in Twickenham, where Alexander Pope also lived.

Clearly there are many ways to improve the unity of this paragraph. Here is just one possibility:

> Horace Walpole was born in 1717 and died in 1797. A Renaissance man, Walpole was an art critic, historian, novelist and politician. From 1741 to 1767 he was a Member of Parliament for Twickenham, following in the footsteps of his father, Robert, who was twice Prime Minister of Great Britain. He lived most of his life in Twickenham (made famous by another renowned man of letters Alexander Pope) in a gothic castle.

As a novelist, Walpole is best known for *The Castle of Otranto. The Castle of Otranto* is a novel of the 'mystery and terror school'. More precisely, it is a 'gothic novel.' Often set in gloomy, isolated castles, gothic novels are characterised by horror, terror, the supernatural and violence, especially murder. *The Castle of Otranto* is about Mandred, the Prince of Otranto. He decides to marry Isabella, the daughter of the Marquis of Vincenza, after Otranto's son (who was betrothed to Isabella) dies under mysterious circumstances. Isabella wants no part of Manfred and runs off, her escape aided by a peasant named Theodore. A series of supernatural events follows, culminating in the collapse of the castle, after which Theodore is declared the rightful heir of Otranto and marries Isabella.

Discussion points

Discuss with your classmates the following thesis statements. Together, compose topic sentences that would probably appear in the body paragraphs of an essay on each topic.

- Some professional athletes are not very good role models.
- Classic novels do not necessarily translate into good movies.
- The quality of the hamburgers varies widely from one fast-food restaurant to the next.
- Some television sitcoms have a lot of situation but not much comedy.

Practical assignment

Read an article in a recently published academic journal which is of interest to you. Closely examine a section, consisting of about five paragraphs, of the body of the paper. Write a three-hundred-word review of this passage, based upon the characteristics of effective body paragraphs discussed in this chapter.

Study and revision tips

Remember that the average length of a body paragraph in an academic essay will be about 150 words. When you revise your essays, make sure your topic sentences are adequately supported.

7 Writing an Explicit Conclusion

One-minute overview

A good academic essay needs a clear and strong conclusion. In an essay of fewer than a thousand words, the conclusion will usually be a single paragraph. In a longer essay or report the conclusion might be longer, its length in proportion to the length of the essay. A hundred-page essay or report might have a ten-page conclusion.

Whatever its length, an effective conclusion must establish a sense of **closure.** The tone and the content of a concluding paragraph or paragraphs must indicate that the essay's purpose has been fulfilled. Readers must recognise an ending when they read it and feel that nothing else needs to be said about the essay's thesis. A concluding paragraph or paragraphs might also **summarise** the content of the body of the essay, and it will often **reaffirm** the thesis. But it must give readers the sense that the writer has fulfilled her obligations: she has said what she had promised she would say.

This chapter presents five examples of concluding paragraphs from academic essays. It also presents an analysis of the effectiveness of each paragraph, based upon the criteria for good conclusions discussed above.

Sample concluding paragraph 1

In summary, there is no independent scientific evidence to support any claim by any cosmetics company that one of their 'miracle creams' performs anything close to miracles. Studies that cosmetic companies refer to in their advertisements are clearly suspect, conducted as they were by dermatologists employed by those same companies and undertaken without the controls that scientific studies must have to be considered valid. Why do millions of women believe the companies' claims? They believe because they want to think they can recapture their youthful beauty. The billion dollar cosmetics industry is a monument to the triumph of vanity and fantasy over science.

Analysis

The introductory phrase 'In summary,' suggests that this is the concluding paragraph of the essay since summaries are generally included at the end. Some teachers are not enthusiastic about concluding paragraphs that begin 'In summary' or 'In conclusion', viewing them as limited and unimaginative. That first sentence also reiterates the essay's thesis, something concluding paragraphs often do. The next sentence reminds readers of key points in the body of the essay. The next sentence is a question, the answer to which is given in the last two sentences. The question is answered unequivocally and with a blunt tone that indicates the essay is finished.

Sample concluding paragraph 2

Eventually, though, Keats would resolve the anguish and torment that comes through so powerfully in 'Ode to a Nightingale'. He would resign himself to the reality of his illness and accept the fact that his illness meant his life would be so very brief. He would come to learn that the truth cannot be ignored, but that, even though the truth does hurt, it does not have to diminish the beauty of life. As he would learn and write in his next poem, 'Ode on a Grecian Urn', 'Beauty is truth, truth beauty'.

Analysis

This is the concluding paragraph to an essay which explicates Keats's poem, 'Ode to a Nightingale'. It concludes the discussion of the poem, then relates the poem to the next one Keats would write. This technique of hinting at a future concern is a common one in concluding paragraphs and is used effectively here. The paragraph also ends with a quotation, another common and effective strategy in a concluding paragraph.

Sample concluding paragraph 3

With networks, writers can revise and edit work collaboratively much more efficiently than they could passing hard copy around a room. With spell checks, writers can correct a word in a fraction of the time it takes to look a word up in an old-fashioned paper dictionary. With grammar checks, writers are cued to correct incomplete or rambling sentences. But computers can't think for themselves or develop a weak idea or make style more graceful. The computer makes writing, as it makes so many of the tasks of life, easier, but it needs the guidance of a human mind to make writing more interesting and intelligent.

Analysis

This is the concluding paragraph from an essay about the benefits and drawbacks of composing on a computer. It provides a good summary of the points presented in the essay, the points in support of computer-based writing and those which express the computer's limitations. In fact, the paragraph is really only summary, though the thesis is implicitly re-stated, and the last sentence, while still part of the summary, does communicate that sense of closure important in concluding paragraphs.

Sample concluding paragraph 4

The American government should not pressure the Honduran government to shut down its sweatshops, nor should it use sanctions to coerce the Hondurans into enacting child labour laws that would prevent children from working in them. A poor wage is better than no wage. Food, shelter and clothing trump education in the hierarchy of human needs. But the

> analysis presented here certainly suggests that the governments of countries whose citizens consume the goods produced in Third World countries could pressure these countries to improve working conditions without provoking the governments of underdeveloped countries into threats of closing down the factories altogether. Americans can continue to exercise their right to enrich celebrity designers by paying top dollar for clothes made by poor 12-year-olds, earning a dollar a day.

Analysis

This concluding paragraph, from an essay about the problem of American clothing manufacturers using underpaid child labour in Third World countries to make their garments, appears to summarise the body of the essay and re-state the thesis. Unfortunately, the thesis is ambiguous. The first part of the paragraph suggests that Americans are benefiting the economy of Honduras by sending them work, even if the workers are young and underpaid by American standards. But the end of the paragraph suggests that Americans are exploiting Third World children. Moreover, the first part of the paragraph suggests that the essay focuses on one country, but, by the end of the paragraph, it seems as if the essay focuses on underdeveloped countries in general. Academic writing should never be ambiguous. Concluding paragraphs, especially, must reflect specifically the content of the essay they are meant to bring to closure.

Sample concluding paragraph 5

> By about 1770, the popularity of the rococo style was fading, even in cities like Prague, Munich, Dresden, and Vienna where it had flourished. Trendsetters were beginning to look upon the asymmetrical ornamentation which was a hallmark of the rococo style as more ungainly and unbalanced than light-hearted and whimsical. Inevitably, rococo would give way to the symmetry of the neoclassical style which would dominate European architecture until the end of the century.

Analysis

This concluding paragraph, from a brief essay tracing the history of rococo architecture, ends, appropriately, by mentioning the year around which the rococo period began to fade. In an essay organised chronologically such an ending is appropriate and effective. Notice as well that, even though the essay is not about the neoclassical style which superseded rococo, the paragraph does mention the transition. This technique of ending an essay by hinting at a future trend or development is common and, as long as the essay topic lends itself to the technique, effective.

Our case study continued

Having drafted her introductory and body paragraphs, Audrey is ready now to draft her conclusion. An effective conclusion reasserts the essay's central idea and establishes a sense of closure. Here is the draft of her concluding paragraph:

> *Many scholars will continue to debunk the notion that the sonnet characters are identifiable, but many readers, especially modern readers so exposed to the gossip of tabloids and television, will continue to enjoy reading the sonnets as autobiographical. A story of sex, deception and jealousy, set amidst the highest social and artistic circles, is bound to arouse interest and cause speculation about the identity of the people who figure in the story. Unless there is a major historical discovery, we will never know who these people truly were, if they were, indeed, real. But Shakespeare scholars will continue to speculate about the identity of W.H., the dark lady, and the rival poet – three people who may have figured very prominently in the life of the greatest of all English poets.*

Audrey's conclusion reasserts her thesis, especially in the paragraph's second sentence, and establishes the sense of closure an essay requires. It is not flashy – a conclusion of an essay about a sonnet sequence might end with a pithy, relevant quote from one of the sonnets – and she may consider revising her conclusion as she revises and edits the rest of her draft.

Tutorial

Progress questions

1. Find five epigrams (an epigram is a common old saying such as 'A rolling stone gathers no moss') which might work effectively as part of a concluding paragraph. Identify the topics of the imaginary essays for which your epigrams might be used effectively.
2. Compose a concluding paragraph which ends by hinting at a future concern related to the essay's topic. See Sample Concluding Paragraph 2 as an example.
3. Compose a concluding paragraph that includes a relevant question.

Discussion points

What are some good rhetorical strategies and techniques to use at the end of an academic essay to alert your readers to the fact that your essay is about to conclude?

Practical assignment

In an essay of approximately 500 words, describe the characteristics of an effective concluding paragraph for an academic essay. Illustrate your description, using three concluding paragraphs (but none of the ones included in this chapter) you believe to be effective.

Study and revision tip

When you are revising a draft of an academic essay, you should check your conclusion to make sure you have reaffirmed your thesis and established that sense of closure that readers expect.

8 Using Cohesive Ties between Sentences and Paragraphs

One-minute overview

A cohesive tie is a word or a phrase that connects a sentence or a paragraph to the sentence or the paragraph which precedes and/or follows it. Cohesive ties help readers follow the writer's train of thought. They signal the nature of the relationships between and among sentences and paragraphs and, in so doing, help make writing clear. Cohesive ties include transitional words and phrases, key words which are repeated throughout a paragraph, synonyms which are substitutes for key words, and pronouns which refer to key words. In other words, you can establish cohesion in your writing through:

- transition
- repetition
- substitution.

Using transitional words and phrases

A transitional word or phrase defines the nature of the relationship between and among sentences and paragraphs. Transitional words and phrases such as 'furthermore', 'in addition', and 'also' suggest that the sentence containing this word or phrase will add something to a previous sentence, something which will provide further related information. Similarly, transitional words or phrases such as 'another', 'a second', and 'a third' suggest that new points will be made. Transitional expressions such as 'consequently' or 'therefore' suggest a cause/effect relationship between two sentences or paragraphs. Transitional words such as 'but' and 'however' signal a contradiction or a contrast between a sentence and the one which follows. And transitionals such as 'meanwhile', 'soon', 'after' and 'later' establish temporal relationships between sentences and the events explained within them. Notice the use of transitional expressions which are highlighted in this passage:

> *The human spinal column is an intricate and complex structure.* ***As a result****, the human back, the lower back especially, is susceptible to trouble.* ***Indeed****, back problems are one of the most common reasons for a visit to the doctor.*
>
> ***One*** *such problem is simple back strain, which typically follows the exercise of muscles which have not been used to so much attention.* ***For example****, back muscles are often put to work for which they are not ready, after the first snowfall of the year, and,* ***consequently****, feel uncommon stress, which leads to mild but still painful inflammation.*
>
> ***Another****, and more serious problem is the so-called 'slipped disc'.* ***Now*** *the discs between each vertebra in the human back are attached to ligaments and cannot, literally, slip. They can,* ***however****, prolapse, which means that a portion of the disc may protrude through the fibres of the ligaments. . . .*

Examine carefully the transitional words and phrases used in the passage above and note how they improve clarity by establishing the relationship between and among the sentences. Read the passage without its transitional words and you will notice the extent to which transitional words and phrases aid clarity.

Using repetition

You can also establish cohesion by repeating a key word or by repeating a particular sentence pattern.

Here is a paragraph which **repeats a key word** to help keep the reader on track:

> *The* ***Sabbath*** *is a Jewish day of rest and worship. After they were sent into exile, Jews proclaimed their identity, in part by insisting upon the holiness of their* ***Sabbath*** *day. Jesus supported the* ***Sabbath*** *in principle, but was vexed by the number of rules needed to keep the* ***Sabbath*** *holy. He refused to honour the* ***Sabbath*** *as a day of rest and, as a result, was condemned by the Pharisees.*

Here is a paragraph which **repeats a sentence pattern** to help establish a sense of coherence:

> *Unfortunately, all forms of government are imperfect. Left-wing governments are strong on social justice but weak on economic prosperity. Right-wing governments are strong on economic prosperity but weak on social justice. In good economic times, left-wing governments should assume power so that wealth is equitably distributed. In bad economic times, right-wing governments should assume power to work their magic on the economy. Under such a shared system, economic prosperity will lead to social justice.*

Notice how the structure of the third sentence in the paragraph above mirrors the structure of the sentence which precedes it. Similarly, the fifth sentence mirrors the structure of the fourth. This creates a sense of balance within the paragraph that helps create the sense that the paragraph sticks together, that it is cohesive.

Using substitution

As you learned earlier in this chapter, coherence can be established in a paragraph by repeating a key word. You do not, of course, want to repeat a key word too many times in the course of a single paragraph because such repetition can make your paragraph appear boring and unimaginative. But what you can and should do is **substitute** the key word with a synonym or with a pronoun that refers back to the key word. Note the use of substitution for the key word 'tourist' to maintain the coherence in the following paragraph:

> *Tourists are instantly recognisable by their physical appearance.* ***They*** *are usually dressed in baggy shorts and souvenir T-shirts, and* ***they*** *usually come armed with camcorders under their arms or hoisted onto their shoulders. These special* ***visitors*** *also have a way of walking that distinguishes them from the locals.* ***They*** *meander quite aimlessly, stopping at every other intersection to gaze up at the street signs or to point their camcorders at buildings, the architectural significance of which usually eludes their hosts. Tourists also tend to have happily vacant facial expressions, in contrast to the grim determination set in the expression of the locals. Still, the locals welcome these* ***alien invaders*** *who can be counted on to boost the local economy.*

Our case study continued

Having written drafts of her introductory, body and concluding paragraphs for her essay about the characters in Shakespeare's sonnets and their real-life counterparts, Audrey must now **revise** her work.

Revision is all about order and substance. It is at this stage in the process that a writer asks these questions:

1. Does my essay have a sound structure? Is the order in which I present my paragraphs logical and effective? Will the order in which I arrange my paragraphs help my readers follow my train of thought?

2. Does my essay have substance? Have I said enough? Do I need to add paragraphs or further develop any I have already drafted?

In her draft, Audrey organised her paragraphs according to the importance of the three characters in the narrator's life. She talks about the patron/friend first because he is the most important character in the story; the dark lady next because she is next in importance and the rival poet last.

Audrey reconsiders and wonders if she should order her paragraphs not according to the size of the characters' roles (patron/friend, dark lady, rival poet) but to the sequence of their appearance in the sonnets: friend, rival poet, dark lady. There is obvious logic to such an order, but there is another advantage as well: she would save the best for last. If she saves her discussion of the identity of the dark lady until the end she will strengthen her essay because the dark lady is the most intriguing of the characters. Good writers, wanting to leave a favourable impression in their readers' minds, usually leave the most interesting aspect of their essay until the end. Audrey decides to change the structure of her essay and place information about the dark lady at the end instead of in the middle.

Re-reading her draft, Audrey also realises she has not quoted from any of the sonnets in support of her ideas. She knows her professor will appreciate quotes used this way, so she plans to look for places quotes might go and for effective quotes to fit into those places.

Re-reading her draft again, Audrey concludes that she needs to put the three characters into a clearer context. She has not really summarised the full story the sonnets tell, and she thinks she must do this to help her readers understand why scholars have identified the characters the way they have. She will add at least one more paragraph summarising the story the sonnets tell.

Tutorial

Progress questions

Revise the following paragraphs to improve their unity and coherence. Add words and combine sentences as needed to create a more readable paragraph.

> Achilles fought at the Trojan War. He had magnificent armour. He was killed. An arrow pierced his heel. His heel was the only vulnerable part of his body. His mother, Thetis, knew the War would endanger Achilles' life. She dipped him, when he was a baby, into the River Styx to protect him from injury. She held him by the heel, which did not get covered in water. Odysseus and Ajax fought over Achilles' armour. Odysseus and Ajax were both fearsome warriors. Odysseus killed Ajax. Years later, Odysseus had occasion to visit the land of the dead. Ajax refused to talk to him.
>
> In September, 1970, Salvador Allende was elected president of Chile. He was the first politician of a non-communist country to run as a Marxist-Leninist and be elected in a free vote. He normalised relations with Cuba. He normalised relations with the People's Republic of China. He nationalised American companies. The military despised his policies. Augusto Pinochet was the Army Chief of Staff. In September, 1973, he led a junta against Allende and seized power.
>
> For years, astronomers did not know much about the planet Mercury. It is, in our solar system, the planet closest to the sun. The most powerful telescopes could not get a good view of Mercury. There was too much glare from the sun to see Mercury clearly. In the mid 70s, NASA launched Mariner 10. It sent photographs of Mercury back to astronomers on Earth. The photos revealed a mountainous planet. It has cliffs two kilometres high and 1500 kilometres long. It contains a crater over 800 miles in diameter. Its surface is covered by a crust of light silicate rock. It is rich in iron.

Clearly there are many ways to improve the unity and coherence of these paragraphs. Here is one possible way of revising the first of the three.

> Achilles fought in the Trojan War. He had magnificent armour to protect him, but he was nevertheless killed when an arrow pierced his heel, the only vulnerable part of his body. Achilles' mother, Thetis, knew the war would endanger Achilles' life, so when he was a baby she dipped him into the River Styx to protect him from injury. But she held him by the heel, which did not get covered by the magical water that would make her son invincible.
>
> After Achilles' death, two other fearsome Trojan War heroes, Odysseus and Ajax, fought over Achilles' armour. Odysseus was victorious and killed Ajax. Years later, returning home after the war had ended, Odysseus had occasion to visit the land of the dead but, not surprisingly, Ajax refused to talk to him.

Discussion Points

1. Why is cohesion important in academic writing?
2. What would you compare an essay without cohesion to?

Practical assignment

Read an article in a popular magazine of interest to you. Study carefully the author's methods of establishing cohesion within his or her article. Write a 300-word account of the author's use of transition, repetition, and substitution as cohesive ties.

Study and revision tips

To check for sound cohesion within an academic essay, read your essay out loud. Your ear might hear a need for cohesion your eye did not see.

9 Avoiding Errors in Sentence Grammar

One-minute overview

Grammar is the study of the order, the function, and the form of words in sentences and of the rules that govern this order, function, and form. Tutors take the rules of English grammar very seriously: they do not like to see grammatical errors in the essays that they mark, and they are likely to penalise an essay that contains grammatical errors. When you revise and edit your academic essays, check your grammar. Make sure, especially, that:

- the case of your pronouns is correct
- your pronouns clearly refer to the nouns to which they are supposed to refer
- your verb tense is correct
- your verbs agree with their subjects.

Pronoun case

There are three types or three **cases** of pronouns: subjective, objective, and possessive. English pronouns divide as follows into their three cases:

Subjective	Objective	Possessive
I	me	my, mine
you	you	your(s)
he	him	his
she	her	her(s)
we	us	our(s)
they	them	their(s)
who	whom	whose
it	it	its

The rules for correct pronoun use are straightforward. Pronouns in the subjective case are used as subjects of verbs: 'He was born in 1795.' Pronouns in the objective case are used as objects of verbs: 'He met her at a flea market'; or as objects of prepositions: 'He knew she was the girl for him.' Pronouns in the possessive case are used to show possession: 'He liked her long blonde hair, and she liked his red braces*.'

*For US readers, in the UK braces are suspenders.

The rules are straightforward, but applying these rules sometimes requires concentration. There are four pronoun pitfalls to avoid.

Pronoun/noun combinations

Be careful when you use a noun and a pronoun together; it is easy to make an error. You are unlikely to make an error if the noun/pronoun combination is acting as a subject: 'Dr Johnson and I met for tea at the Strand.' But remember that you must use the objective case if the pronoun is the object of a verb, even if it is in combination with a noun: 'The staff at the Strand expected Dr Johnson and me to come for tea every Thursday afternoon.' And, similarly, you must use the objective case of the pronoun if the pronoun is the object of a preposition, even if the pronoun is used in combination with a noun: 'The staff at the Strand wanted to know who was coming with Dr Johnson and me.' If this use of the objective case of the pronoun sounds wrong to you, eliminate the noun and you will know immediately that the objective case must be right: they are expecting me; they want to know who is coming with me.

Pronouns in a comparison

When you use a pronoun in a comparison, complete the comparison (in your mind if not in the text) and you will select the correct pronoun. If you write 'She reads poetry more often than me', you are saying she reads poetry more than me does, when you obviously mean more than I do. In fact, if you write 'She reads poetry more often than me', you are saying she reads poetry more often than she reads me. Indeed, pronouns in comparisons can cause such confusion. If you write: 'My mother likes mushrooms more than me', you are saying your mother likes mushrooms more than she likes you. If you mean to say she likes mushrooms more than you like mushrooms, change the me to I.

Who and whom

'Who' is the subjective case of the pronoun, and 'whom' is the objective case. 'Who', then, is used as a subject of a verb: 'I know who is coming with you.' 'Who' is the subject of the verb 'is coming'.

'Whom' is used as the object of a verb: 'Dr Johnson did not know whom he could trust'. 'Whom' is the object of the verb 'could trust'. That verb already has a subject, 'he', so the subjective pronoun 'who' could not be used.

'Whom' is also used as the object of a preposition: 'I think you know that journalist with whom Dr Johnson is speaking.' Can you also write: 'I think you know that journalist whom Dr Johnson is speaking with'? To do so puts the preposition at the end of the sentence. Many academics think the rule about never ending a sentence with a preposition is archaic and they will not penalise essays which contain such sentences. Some academics, however, still think that ending a sentence with a preposition is a solecism, and they may penalise such a sentence.

'Whom' used as the object of a verb causes more problems than 'whom' used as the object of a preposition. Remember that if the clause needs a subject 'who' is correct; if the clause needs an object 'whom' is correct. Compare these two sentences, both of which are grammatically correct:

We all know whom you believe.
We all know who you believe is telling the truth.

Do you see the difference between them? In the first sentence 'whom' is correct because it is the object of the verb 'believe'. In the second sentence 'who' is correct because it is the subject of the verb 'is telling'.

It's and its

'Its' is a possessive pronoun, and 'it's' is a contraction for 'it is'. These two words are often confused because we indicate possession by adding an apostrophe, and therefore we might reason that 'it's' indicates possessive. It does not. It is only a contraction for 'it is'. Never use 'it's' as the possessive form of the pronoun 'it'. Remember this sentence: 'It's a good movie though I didn't like its ending.'

Pronoun reference

Pronouns replace nouns. The noun the pronoun replaces is called the **antecedent** of that pronoun. Make sure your pronouns cannot refer to more than one antecedent. In this sentence, for example, 'The President hoped to meet the Prime Minister in Madrid but, fearing an assassination attempt, she did not show up', the pronoun 'she' (assuming both the President and the Prime Minister are women) could refer to either the President or the PM. You would have to revise this sentence to clarify the identity of 'she'.

Similarly, you must correct sentences which contain a pronoun which does not appear to have any antecedent at all. In this sentence, 'There was a vigorous debate in the house but MPs knew the House would not agree to it', the pronoun 'it' has no apparent antecedent. Change 'it' to 'the bill' or 'the resolution' or 'the amendment' – whatever the pronoun is supposed to refer to – unless a previous sentence has made absolutely clear what the pronoun's antecedent is.

When you revise your essays, check all of your pronouns to make certain their antecedents are never ambiguous.

Verb tense and mood

Verbs express action, and verb forms or **tenses** change to indicate if that action is taking place in the present, has taken place in the past, or will take place in the future. It is essential that the verb tenses you choose clearly indicate when the action that the verb expresses occurred. Tense is dictated by logic and choosing the correct tense is, therefore, usually quite straightforward. There are, however, a few common errors you must avoid in the selection of your verb tenses.

Past tense of irregular verbs

Verbs typically add the suffix 'ed' to indicate past tense: 'She attended Cambridge University.' When an auxiliary or helping verb precedes the past tense, the form of the past tense (called the **past participle** when preceded by an auxiliary verb) remains the same: 'She has attended Cambridge University for the past three years.'

There are some verbs, however, called **irregular verbs**, which indicate past tense by changing a vowel: 'I gave you my phone number already, and I will not give it to you again.' Complicating matters even further, irregular verbs often have a third form which must be used when such verbs are preceded by an auxiliary or helping verb. In other words, the past participle form of an irregular verb might be different from its past tense form: 'I have given you my phone number already.'

Be careful with irregular verbs. Make sure you use the correct past tense and past participle forms of irregular verbs: 'It breaks my heart to know he broke your heart because my heart has been broken before.' If you are not sure if the verb you are using has an irregular past and past participle form, simply look the verb up in the dictionary. In the *Concise Oxford Dictionary*, for example, the entry for the verb 'freeze' is followed immediately by its past tense and past participle (froze, frozen) forms.

Using the perfect verb form

Sentences with more than one verb often require more than one verb tense: 'She knows she saw him last Tuesday'; 'I know you will win.' As is the case with single-verb sentences, logic dictates tense, and therefore you will not usually make a tense error: 'I know now, in the present, that you will win, at some point in the future.'

But be careful using the **perfect** form of the verb, which is the form preceded by the auxiliary verbs 'has', 'had', or 'have'. You may write: 'She claims she has seen *Gone With the Wind* 27 times.' Or you may write: 'She claims she saw *Gone With the Wind* 27 times.' But there is a subtle difference in meaning between the two sentences. The first sentence, which uses the perfect form of the verb (has seen), implies that she might see the film again. The second sentence, which uses the simple past (saw) suggests she will not. The perfect verb form indicates such subtle differences in meaning.

Similarly, there is a subtle, but important difference between these two sentences.

She was certain she saw him in the audience.
She was certain she had seen him in the audience.

The first sentence implies that she is there at the time of the seeing. The second sentence implies that she is no longer there but is remembering seeing him at an earlier time.

Finally, consider the difference in meaning between these two sentences:

She will attend college next autumn if she earns enough money.
She will attend college next autumn if she has earned enough money.

The first sentence suggests that the earning will take place at a specific time: 'She will attend college next autumn if she earns enough money this summer.' The second sentence does not suggest a specific time when the earning will take place: 'She will attend college next autumn if she has earned enough money by then.'

When you are revising your academic essays, check your verbs, especially your perfect-tense verbs to make certain they express your meaning precisely.

Subjunctive mood

In addition to conveying tense, verbs convey mood. Verb mood describes the attitude a sentence is conveying. Sentences like 'Shut the door!' or 'Get out of my way!' are expressing an imperative attitude and are said to be in the **imperative mood**. Note that the subject (you) is understood, not stated explicitly.

Most verbs indicate a neutral attitude. Such verbs are said to be in the **indicative mood.**

The **subjunctive mood** is used to express a condition contrary to fact, a conjecture, a wish, a recommendation, a demand, or an indirect request. In its present tense, the subjunctive mood is formed by using the uninflected or **infinitive** form of the verb. You would normally write, for example, 'She sees a psychiatrist once a month.' But if that sentence were preceded by a demand, its tense would change to indicate subjunctive mood: 'Her doctor insisted she see a psychiatrist every month.'

In its past tense, the subjunctive mood usually requires the 'were' form of the verb 'to be': 'If she were the Prime Minister, she would raise taxes.' However, some tutors would not penalise the use of 'was' in such sentences. The rule prescribing the use of 'were' to indicate the subjunctive mood is less absolute than it once was.

Subject–verb agreement

Singular subjects take singular verbs – a poet paints with words. Plural subjects take plural verbs – poets paint with words. Usually, subject–verb agreement is that simple. You will write some sentences, however, which will require a moment's thought before you choose the verb form you need to use.

When words intervene between the subject and the verb

If words come between the subject and the verb, be careful not to agree the verb with one of those words. The subject of this sentence – 'One of my books is out of print' – is 'One' which is why the singular form of the verb 'is' is used. My books are out of print, but one of my books is out of print.

When the verb precedes the subject

You might write a sentence in which the verb precedes its subject. In this sentence, for example, the verb 'are' comes well before the subject 'philosophers': 'There are many more important nineteenth century philosophers whose work we did not study.' The verb must be the plural 'are', not the singular 'is', because the subject 'philosophers' is plural.

When the subject is an indefinite pronoun

An indefinite pronoun is one which replaces an indefinite or an inexact noun as opposed to a specific noun: another, anybody, anyone, anything, each, either, every, everybody, everyone, everything, neither, nobody, no one, nothing, somebody, someone, something. Indefinite pronouns usually require the singular form of the verb: 'Neither of my tutors is available on Fridays.'

The indefinite pronouns 'both' and 'many' are always plural: 'Both of my tutors are available on Fridays.'

The indefinite pronouns 'all', 'any', 'more', 'most', 'none', and 'some' can take either singular or plural verbs, the choice being dependent upon the context: 'All of the money is missing, but all of the employees are safe.'

When the noun following the verb is different in number from the subject

Be careful when you have a singular subject followed by a verb followed by a plural noun, as in this sentence: 'The worst part about writing an academic essay is all the grammar rules you need to know.' Because the noun 'rules' is plural, you might be tempted to use the plural verb 'are' instead of the correct verb 'is', but remember it is the subject the verb must agree with. If you have a plural subject followed by a singular noun as in this sentence – 'The rules of English grammar are a problem for me' – the same condition applies. Do not use the singular noun 'is' because it is followed by a singular noun 'problem.' The plural verb 'are' is required because the subject 'rules' is plural.

Collective noun as subject

A collective noun is one that identifies a group: family, team, orchestra, class, audience. Usually, a collective noun takes a singular verb: 'The press is not welcome.' If the collective noun is not acting as a unit, you may use the plural form of the verb: The press are arguing about who will get the interview.

Tutorial

Progress questions

Each of the following sentences contains an error in grammar. Correct the error. Be prepared to explain why you made the correction as you did.

1. If I was a rich man, I would donate money to my alma mater.
2. The professor who I had last year for Russian history has retired.
3. One of my friends want to buy a Porsche.
4. They expected my wife and I to arrive before noon.
5. Dr Smyth gave John and he a difficult assignment.
6. The community welcomed my family but not they.
7. The university admitted Raj but not she.
8. Robert is coming for Jason and I tomorrow night.
9. The boy who she danced with was too short for her.
10. Matt Damon is a much better actor than him.
11. Neither of these sentences are correct.
12. At the Olympic games in Sydney, my sister bought some wonderful pins for her Shauna and I.
13. She says she will go to the winter games in Utah with her boyfriend and they.
14. Eric is quite a bit taller than her.
15. Most students did not do as well on the third test as me.
16. The candidate who I voted for did not give a very good speech at the convention.
17. The candidate who I gave a large donation to won by a landslide.
18. Each of my body paragraphs contain a good topic sentence.
19. Strategies for developing a good body paragraph is discussed in Chapter Four.
20. Each of these sentences are incorrect.
21. Every one of these sentences are incorrect.
22. Neither of these teachers were willing to help me.
23. None of the police officers understand why the judge gave her such a harsh sentence.

24 The entire orchestra refuse to play any more of Mozart's symphonies.

Here are the corrected versions of the sentences above:

1 If I were a rich man, I would donate money to my alma mater.

2 The professor whom I had last year for Russian history has retired.

3 One of my friends wants to buy a Porsche.

4 They expected my wife and me to arrive before noon.

5 Dr. Smyth gave John and him a difficult assignment.

6 The community welcomed my family but not them.

7 The university admitted Raj but not her.

8 Robert is coming for Jason and me tomorrow night.

9 The boy whom she danced with was too short for her.

10 Matt Damon is a much better actor than he.

11 Neither of these sentences is correct.

12 At the Olympic games in Sydney, my sister bought some wonderful pins for her Shauna and me.

13 She says she will go to the winter games in Utah with her boyfriend and them.

14 Eric is quite a bit taller than she.

15 Most students did not do as well on the third test as I.

16 The candidate whom I voted for did not give a very good speech at the convention.

17 The candidate whom I gave a large donation to won by a landslide.

18 Each of my body paragraphs contains a good topic sentence.

19 Strategies for developing a good body paragraph are discussed in Chapter Four.

20 Each of these sentences is incorrect.

21 Every one of these sentences is incorrect.

22 Neither of these teachers was willing to help me.

23 None of the police officers understands why the judge gave her such a harsh sentence.

24 The entire orchestra refuses to play any more of Mozart's symphonies.

Discussion points

1 Why is it important to use correct grammar in academic writing?

2 In what type of writing, if any, is it acceptable to violate the rules of good grammar?

Practical assignment

Identify the grammatical error which has given you some trouble in the past. In an essay of 500–750 words, describe this error and discuss strategies writers can use to avoid and correct it.

Study and revision tip

Ask someone who is knowledgeable about grammar to proofread your work before you give it to your teacher or professor.

10 Avoiding Errors in Sentence Structure

One-minute overview

A sentence is a unit of communication which describes at least one act (in the verb) and one agent (the subject) undertaking that action: 'Alice is working.' Usually, sentences also include phrases and other clauses which develop the subject and the verb: 'Alice is working on her French essay, which is due tomorrow morning.' Because sentences contain a variety of words, phrases, and clauses, sentence structure can become complex and susceptible to error. Before you hand your essays in to your teachers, check the structure of each sentence. You will probably lose a mark if a sentence in your essay is incomplete, awkward, improperly punctuated, or ambiguous. Watch, especially, for those errors in sentence structure which often weaken student writing:

- sentence fragments
- run-on sentences
- misplaced/dangling modifiers
- faulty parallelism
- wordiness.

Sentence fragments

A sentence fragment is an incomplete sentence masquerading as a complete one.

A sentence must contain a subject and a verb and is a fragment if one of these elements is missing. For example:

Alice is busy tonight. Working on her French essay.

'Working on her French essay' cannot be a sentence because it does not contain a subject. It is a sentence fragment. It should be attached to the preceding sentence. A comma should replace the full stop:

Alice is busy tonight, working on her French essay.

A work group can contain a subject and a verb but still be a fragment:

Alice will be working on her French essay all night. Because it is due in her first class tomorrow morning.

The word group 'Because it is due in her first class tomorrow morning' does contain a subject and a verb but is not a complete sentence. It is not a complete sentence because it begins with the word 'because' which is one of those words which introduce subordinate or dependent clauses. A subordinate or dependent clause does contain a subject and a verb, but cannot stand alone: it 'depends' upon, it is 'subordinate' to, a main clause (which is synonymous to a complete sentence). Therefore, the subordinate clause should be a part of the sentence:

Alice will be working on her French essay all night, because it is due in her first class tomorrow morning.

It is also acceptable to put the subordinate clause at the beginning of the sentence, though minor alterations should be made to it:

Because her French essay is due in her first class tomorrow morning, Alice will be working on it all night.

Other words which introduce subordinate or dependent

clauses include 'when', 'if', 'since', 'who', 'whose', 'that', 'which', 'before', 'after', and 'while'. You should learn these words. You should check to make sure these words are within a sentence and do not begin a fragment, when you use them in your essays. Note that if I had punctuated the last sentence like this – 'You should check to make sure these words are within a sentence and do not begin a fragment. When you use them in your essays.' – I would have made a sentence fragment error.

Let's look at one more example. The second sentence in the following pair of sentences is also a fragment:

> *Alice is working on her French essay tonight. The last paper that she needs to hand in to complete the course requirements.*

To correct this fragment, you would have to make it a complete sentence:

> *This is the last paper that she needs to hand in to complete the course requirements.*

Or you would have to attach it to the main clause:

> *Tonight Alice is working on her French essay, which is the last paper that she needs to hand in to complete the course requirements.*

Note that the word introducing the dependent clause, the word 'that,' could be left out, because its presence in the sentence is implicit.

Professional writers will occasionally use a fragment deliberately, usually for emphasis:

The Prime Minister refused to attend the King's funeral. What an insult! To the King's nation as well as to our own.

The last two word groups are fragments but acceptable because they are used deliberately, for emphasis. When writing an academic essay, however, it is best to play it safe and avoid fragments altogether.

The run-on sentence

A run-on sentence consists of two complete sentences incorrectly joined together, usually by a comma. It is certainly acceptable to join two sentences together to make one, but the merger must be done correctly.

Two complete sentences can **not** be separated from each other merely by a comma. Here is an example of a run-on sentence:

Alice is working on her French essay tonight, she can't come to the match.

Clearly there are two separate sentences here, joined together, incorrectly, by a comma. There are several ways to correct a run-on sentence.

You may replace the comma with a full stop or, if the two sentences are related, with a semi-colon. A comma is not considered a strong enough pause to separate two sentences, but a semi-colon is.

You may place a coordinate conjunction ('and', 'but', 'or') after the comma:

Alice is working on her French essay tonight, and she can't come to the match.

You may change one of the sentences into a dependent (subordinate) clause:

> *Since Alice is working on her French essay tonight, she can't come to the match.*

You may, if both subjects refer to the same person, add a coordinate conjunction and eliminate the second subject. Note that if you eliminate the second subject, you also dispense with the comma:

> *Alice is working on her French essay tonight and can't come to the match.*

Note, also, that this solution is not always a possibility. You would need to correct this run-on sentence:

> *Alice is working on her French essay tonight, it is due first period tomorrow.*

using one of the other methods. You could change the comma to a full stop or a semi-colon. Or you could reduce one of the sentences to a subordinate (dependent) clause:

> *Alice is working on her French essay tonight, because it is due first period tomorrow. Tonight Alice is working on her French essay, which is due first period tomorrow.*

Here is one more example. The first sentence is a run-on, because it uses only a comma to separate two complete sentences. The sentences below it illustrate ways of correcting the run-on.

> ✗ *Another common error in sentence structure is the run-on* **sentence, a run**-*on sentence consists of two complete sentences*

joined together by a comma.

✓ *Another common error in sentence structure is the run-on* **sentence. A** *run-on sentence consists of two complete sentences joined together by a comma.*

✓ *Another common error in sentence structure is the run-on* **sentence; a** *run-on sentence consists of two complete sentences joined together by a comma.*

✓ *Another common error in sentence structure is the run-on* **sentence, which** *consists of two complete sentences joined together by a comma.*

✓ *Another common error in sentence structure is the run-on* **sentence, consisting** *of two complete sentences joined together by a comma.*

Note especially, the last method of correction. The second sentence has been reduced not to a subordinate (or dependent) clause, as the sentence above it has, but to a phrase, introduced by the participle 'consisting'. This is another effective method of correcting a run-on sentence.

Misplaced and dangling modifiers

Modifiers are words and phrases which describe, clarify, and refine subjects and verbs and other key elements (usually other nouns and verbs) within sentences. You must be careful to place your modifiers carefully within your sentences so that they clearly modify what you intend them to modify.

A misplaced modifier is a word or group of words which describes a word in a sentence other than the word it is supposed to describe. In this sentence, for example – 'I was able to find two books and several articles in the library that will be useful to me' – the phrase 'that will be useful to me' is misplaced because it modifies 'library' but is meant to modify 'two books and several articles'. Now if the sentence were revised to read 'I was able to find two books and several articles that will be useful to me in the library' we still have a misplaced modifier, in this case the phrase 'in the library', implying as it does that the books and articles will be useful to me in the library but not necessarily anywhere else. If the phrase 'in the library' is placed at the beginning of the sentence, the error is corrected:

In the library, I was able to find two books and several articles that will be useful to me.

Similarly, if the same phrase is placed after the infinitive 'to find', the error is corrected:

I was able to find, in the library, two books and several articles that will be useful to me.

Here is another example. Consider this sentence: 'The future of the Earth relies almost entirely on the sun, a massive ball of flaming gas 330,000 times as large as the Earth, which is slowly running out of energy.' The last clause modifies 'Earth', but the writer intends it to modify 'sun'. A misplaced modifier often indicates that the sentence containing it is too long, and sometimes the best way to correct a misplaced modifier is to compose two shorter sentences:

The sun is a massive ball of flaming gas 330,000 times as large as the Earth. The future of the Earth relies almost entirely on the sun, which is slowly running out of energy.

A dangling modifier is a word or a group of words which is supposed to modify a word in a sentence, but that needed word is missing from the sentence. In this sentence, for example – 'When writing an essay, the rules for good writing should be kept in mind' – the phrase 'When writing an essay' dangles at the beginning, in search of a word it can modify. But there is no such word in the sentence. In fact, it sounds as if 'the rules' are writing the essay. The sentence needs to be revised to give 'When writing an essay' a word it will clearly modify. Here are two possibilities:

When writing an essay, writers should keep in mind the rules for good writing.
When you are writing an essay, you should keep the rules for good writing in mind.

Here is another example:

Looking at present trends in carbon dioxide levels in the air, predictions can be made that levels will drop to 140 parts per million in five hundred million years.

Predictions cannot look at present trends. Astronomers can, though. Therefore, the sentence should be revised to read:

Looking at present trends in carbon dioxide levels in the air, astronomers can predict that levels will drop to 140 parts per million in five hundred million years.

Misplaced and dangling modifiers make sentences ambiguous. When you are revising your essay, check the placement of your modifiers to make sure they do not make any of your sentences awkward or unclear.

Faulty parallelism

Faulty parallelism is an error in sentence structure that occurs when a word or phrase in a sentence is expressed in a different part of speech than other words or phrases that are in the same section of the sentence. Faulty parallelism adversely affects the balance of a sentence. This sentence – 'He managed to make the team even though he is short, awkward, and weight is a problem for him, as well' – lacks parallelism because the phrase 'weight is a problem for him, as well' does not balance the adjectives 'short' and 'awkward'. The sentence would be parallel if the phrase were changed to the adjective 'overweight'.

Here is another example of faulty parallelism:

> *The company will either go bankrupt or there was a leveraged buyout possibility that could save it.*

'Go bankrupt' does not balance 'there was'; 'be saved' would be a much better match. We could, then establish a parallel structure and make the sentence more fluent with this revision:

> *The company will either* **go bankrupt** *or* **be saved** *by a leveraged buyout.*

Wordiness

The structure of some sentences appears shaky because the writer has used more words than necessary to express the ideas the sentence contains. Here is an example of a wordy sentence:

> *This essay will explore several different theories that have been developed by paleontologists for attempting to explain why dinosaurs reached the point of becoming extinct.*

Read the sentence out loud and you will hear the wordiness. The first half is not too bad; the second half is a wordy disaster, especially 'reached the point of becoming extinct', which could be reduced simply to 'became extinct'. The sentence could be revised as follows:

This essay will explore several theories paleontologists have developed to explain why dinosaurs became extinct.

Some teachers will not even like the 'This essay will explore,' on the grounds that it is already implied. They might favour an even more concise version of the sentence:

Paleontologists have developed several theories to explain why dinosaurs became extinct.

Wordiness is a matter of degree, to a certain extent. You want your sentences to be concise but complete.

Here is another example of a wordy sentence:

In 1916, the disease of polio reached epidemic proportions when 27,363 cases of polio were reported by health care workers in America and more than 7000 people died of polio as a result in the worst outbreak of polio in the history of the country.

Again, read the sentence out loud and the need for concision is apparent. 'The disease of' is unnecessary; it is not necessary to repeat 'polio' three times; 'as a result' is implied. The sentence could be half as long and say the same thing more eloquently:

In 1916, American health care workers reported 27,363 cases of polio and over 7000 deaths, in the country's worst polio epidemic.

One of the enemies of concision in both of the above wordy

sentences is the **passive voice,** in the phrases 'have been developed' in the first and 'were reported' in the second. The passive voice is a form of a verb which adds part of the verb 'to be' to a past participle: 'was thrown', 'is forbidden', 'am disappointed'. The passive voice tends to be wordy. This sentence – 'The ball was thrown by my brother' – is more wordy than this sentence – 'My brother threw the ball.' The passive voice is not wrong; indeed, it is useful if the subject of the sentence is indeterminate: 'Smoking is forbidden in this building.' (Who is doing the forbidding?) But the passive voice is wordy when there is a word in the sentence that should be the subject but is stuck somewhere else, usually as the object in a prepositional phrase. There is nothing wrong with this sentence, for example – 'Three of the goals were scored by defencemen' – but it is less concise than this sentence – 'Defencemen scored three of the goals.'

Tutorial

Progress questions

Identify the error in sentence structure in each of the following sentences and revise each sentence to correct the error. Some sentences will require minor revisions; others will require major revisions.

1. The Berlin Wall was built in the early 1960s. Dividing the eastern part of Berlin into a communist sector and the western part of the city into a capitalist sector.
2. The Aardvark is a nocturnal mammal about one and a half metres long, it feeds on termites and ants.
3. Acid rain is rain that contains too much acid, especially too much acidity which is found in the nitric acid and the sulphuric acid which are components of acid rain.
4. While he was Secretary General of the United Nations, Dag Hammarskjold worked tirelessly for peace in the Middle

and East and the Congo, and the Nobel Prize for peace was awarded to him in 1962.

5 Alan is planning to attend the local junior college, Chris is going to university, while the decision Jenny has made is to go to work in her mother's business.

6 By the end of the movie, the main character has become quite unstable, losing his identity and, ultimately, he commits suicide.

7 Sports psychologists feel that some athletes take steroids not so much because they crave victory but it is from having low self-esteem.

8 After waiting for over an hour, the concert finally began.

9 To survive a winter in Winnipeg, warm clothing and patience are essential.

10 The candidate gave the same speech opposing the bill in every town in the country.

11 I gave my old copy of the text to my friend with all of the exercises completed.

12 I thought I might be fired after I refused to pour coffee for the truckers in their own thermoses.

13 Professor Higgins collected all of the assignments about the civil war on Friday.

14 Passengers may not take a suitcase onto a plane that won't fit into the overhead compartment.

15 The bicycle we found at the dump that is missing its handle bars can easily be repaired.

16 While trying to sneak into the house past curfew, a vase crashed to the floor.

17 An old man accompanied my wife whom I had never seen before.

18 Americans were at first puzzled and then annoyed. When the Toronto Blue Jays won the world series.

19 After the Second World War, the demand for public education increased dramatically. Mainly as a result of the

baby boom.

20 Cats have excellent vision, they can see as well at night as they can during the day.

21 Leonard Cohen was an influential song writer, especially during the 1960s, his songs were recorded by artists in several different countries.

22 A contract is an agreement between two people to allow for the exchange of goods and services, one person provides a product of a service, the other person pays for it.

23 Psychotherapy is not a single method of treating mental illness but a term that encompasses many other types of therapies for treating mental illness using a variety of methods.

24 A black hole is a star that has such a strong gravitational force that nothing can escape its gravitational pull, including light which is why a black hole cannot be seen and its existence is speculated upon.

Here are the corrected versions of the above sentences. Note that there are other methods of correcting these sentences besides the ones presented here:

1 The Berlin Wall was built at the end of World War II, dividing the eastern part of Berlin into a communist sector and the western part of the city into a capitalist sector.

2 The aardvark is a nocturnal mammal about 1.5 metres long. It feeds on termites and ants.

3 Acid rain contains too much nitric and sulphuric acid.

4 While he was Secretary General of the United Nations, Dag Hammarskjold worked tirelessly for peace in the Middle East and the Congo, and he won the Nobel Prize for peace in 1962.

5 Alan is planning to attend the local junior college, Chris is going to the state university, while Jenny has decided to go to work in her mother's business.

6 By the end of the movie, the main character has become quite unstable, losing his identity and, ultimately,

committing suicide.

7 Sports psychologists feel that some athletes take steroids not so much because they crave victory but because they have low self-esteem.

8 After we had waited for over an hour, the concert finally began.

9 To survive a winter in Winnipeg, residents need warm clothing and patience.

10 In every town in the country, the candidate gave the same speech opposing the bill.

11 I gave my old copy of the text, with all of the exercises completed, to my friend.

12 I thought I might be fired after I refused to pour, in their own thermoses, coffee for the truckers.

13 On Friday, Professor Higgins collected all of the assignments about the civil war.

14 Passengers may not take a suitcase that won't fit into the overhead compartment onto a plane.

15 The bicycle, missing its handlebars, we found at the dump can easily be repaired.

16 While we were trying to sneak into the house past curfew, a vase crashed to the floor.

17 An old man whom I had never seen before accompanied my wife.

18 Americans were at first puzzled and then annoyed, when the Toronto Blue Jays won the World Series.

19 After the Second World War, the demand for public education increased dramatically, mainly as a result of the baby boom.

20 Cats have excellent vision. They can see as well at night as they can during the day.

21 Leonard Cohen was an influential song writer, especially during the 1960s. His songs were recorded by artists in several different countries.

22 A contract is an agreement between two people to allow for the exchange of goods and services. One person provides a product or a service, the other person pays for it.

23 Psychotherapy is not a single method of treating mental illness but one that encompasses many other types of therapies.

24 A black hole is a star that has such a strong gravitational force that nothing, including light, can escape its gravitational pull. For this reason, a black hole cannot be seen and its existence is speculative.

Discussion points

1 What is the difference between a misplaced and a dangling modifier?

2 When is it acceptable to use a sentence fragment?

Practical assignment

Select the error in sentence structure that has given you some trouble in your own writing. In an essay of approximately 500 words, describe the error, provide examples, and discuss ways of correcting it.

Study and revision tip

If you think a sentence you have written might contain a structural error, but you are not sure, remove the sentence from the paragraph and study it outside its rhetorical context. Sometimes it is easier to spot errors in structure in this way.

11 Writing With Style

One-minute overview

Academic writing should be clear and straightforward, but there is no reason why it should be dull. An interesting subject makes an interesting essay, but that interest will be diminished if the information is conveyed in a dull writing style. A dull writing style is characterised mainly by a series of short, choppy sentences joined together, if at all, by conjunctions such as 'and'. A short, simple sentence does not make a dull style. Indeed, a short, simple sentence can be used effectively, especially to emphasise a particular point. What you want to avoid in your writing is a **series** of short, choppy sentences, which make your writing sound as if it were written by a ten-year-old or by an untalented journalist.

The key to avoiding a passage of dull sentences is to read your essay out loud while you are revising it. If you have written a passage consisting of too many short, dull sentences, you will be able to hear the problem (as will your reader), and you can make the necessary revisions to make your style more pleasing. There are a variety of ways to vary your sentence structure and thereby improve your writing style. Three common and effective methods are:

- using subordination to combine a series of short choppy sentences
- establishing parallelism within a sentence
- varying the order of words and phrases in a sentence.

Using subordination

If you have written a series of three or four short, choppy sentences, you might want to combine them into two or even one more interesting and sophisticated sentence by changing some of the sentences into clauses or phrases and adding those clauses or phrases on to one complete sentence. This process is called subordination. The writer takes one sentence and changes it into a phrase or a clause and attaches the phrase or clause to a complete sentence. The phrase or clause thereby becomes 'subordinate' to the main clause, the complete sentence.

Let's look at an example. Consider this passage:

> *The word discreet is an adjective. It means prudent or modest. Here is a sentence which uses the word* discreet *correctly: 'He was too discreet to reveal her age.' The word discrete is also an adjective. But spelled this way it means separate or distinct. Here is an example. 'We are officially part of their department, but we operate as a discrete entity.'*

This is an informative paragraph, but its pedestrian style has a somnolent effect on the reader and detracts from the interesting information the paragraph contains. A more interesting version of the same paragraph might read:

> *The word discreet is an adjective, which means prudent or modest, as in the sentence: 'He was too discreet to reveal her age.' The word discrete is also an adjective, but, spelled this way, it means separate or distinct, as in the sentence: 'We are officially part of their department, but we operate as a discrete entity.'*

This version has a rhythm and flow that signals a more mature writing style and makes the paragraph more authoritative. What accounts for the improvement in the style of this paragraph?

The second sentence has been subordinated into a clause, the third sentence has been subordinated into a phrase and both have been attached (with a comma) to the first sentence. The same process has been repeated with the fourth, fifth, and sixth sentences.

Let's look at one more example. Here is a paragraph written in an uninspired style, consisting, as it does, of a succession of short, choppy sentences.

> *William Penn was an English Quaker. His father was a prominent admiral. The British government gave Penn a large tract of land in the new colony of America. They gave him the land in recognition of his father's naval career. Penn decided to establish a Quaker colony in America. In 1681, Penn and his cousin, William Markham, went to America. They were accompanied by a group of hearty Quaker colonists. They made their way to the junction of the Schuylkill and Delaware Rivers. Here they founded a City of Brotherly Love. This city eventually became Philadelphia. It became the capital of the state named after William Penn.*

Here is the same paragraph revised to improve its sentence variety.

> *William Penn was an English Quaker, the son of a prominent admiral. The British government gave Penn a large tract of land in the new colony of America, in recognition of his father's naval career. Penn decided to establish a Quaker colony in America. In 1681, Penn and his cousin, William Markham, journeyed to America, accompanied by a group of hearty Quaker colonists. They made their way to the junction of the Schuylkill and Delaware Rivers, where they founded a City of Brotherly Love. This city eventually became Philadelphia, the capital of the state named after William Penn.*

The first version of the paragraph is not incorrect, but an adult reader would likely find it juvenile and dull. The revised version is more readable because, through subordination, the choppy sentence structure has been replaced with sentences that have a better sense of rhythm and flow.

Effective parallelism

As a term in written composition, parallelism describes a sentence within which words, phrases, or clauses complement each other and create a sense of rhythm and balance within the sentence. (In Chapter 9, you learned about faulty parallelism, an error in sentence structure that occurs when a word or phrase in a sentence is expressed in a different part of speech than other words or phrases that are in the same section of the sentence.) Effective parallelism can create a graceful and striking sentence. Note the use of parallel structure in this excerpt from Winston Churchill's speech to the House of Commons on 8 October 1940. He was speaking about Great Britain's participation in the Second World War:

> *Death and sorrow will be the companions of our journey; hardship our garment; constancy and valour our only shield. We must be united, we must be undaunted, we must be inflexible.*

Without parallelism, the passage would lose much of its strength:

> *Death and sorrow will be the companions of our journey. We will also experience much hardship which we will have to endure. We will have to shield ourselves with constancy and valour. We must be united. We cannot let our enemy frighten us. We must be inflexible.*

This version is grammatically correct, but it lacks the passion, the concision, and emphasis of the original because Churchill's effective use of parallelism has been replaced by short, rather dull sentences.

Here is another example, this time from President Kennedy's inaugural address made on 20 January 1961:

Let the word go forth from this time and place, to friend and foe alike, that the torch has been passed to a new generation of Americans, born in this century, tempered by war, disciplined by a hard and bitter peace, proud of our ancient heritage, and unwilling to witness or permit the slow undoing of those human rights to which this nation has always been committed, and to which we are committed today at home and around the world.

Let every nation know, whether it wishes us well or ill, that we shall pay any price, bear any burden, meet any hardship, support any friend, oppose any foe to assure the survival and the success of liberty.

Without the parallel structure Kennedy uses so effectively, this passage loses that stirring tone which complements the author's forthright message:

Let the word go forth from this time and place, to friend and foe alike, that the torch has been passed to a new generation of Americans. These Americans were born in this century, and they have been tempered by war. In addition, they have been disciplined by a hard and bitter peace. They are proud of our ancient heritage, and unwilling to witness or permit the slow undoing of those human rights to which this nation has always been committed. We will remain committed to these rights today at home and around the world.

Let every nation know, whether it wishes us well or ill, that we shall pay any price to assure the survival and the success of liberty. Furthermore, we will bear any burden and meet any hardship in the interest of the same cause. Finally, we will support any friend, oppose any foe to assure the survival and the success of liberty.

In summary, then, the use of parallel structure can improve a writing style by making it at once more concise and more dramatic.

Using word order effectively

Most English sentences are structured so that a subject follows a verb:

> *Their debate was typical. The Labour candidate promised to increase public spending on education and health care, to win the votes of working families. The Conservative promised to lower taxes, to win the votes of the business community.*

You can make your writing style, and, hence, your message, more interesting if, on occasion, you deviate from the standard 'subject-follows-a-verb' pattern at the beginning of a sentence.

> *Their debate was typical. To win the votes of working families, the Labour candidate promised to increase public spending on education and health care. To win the votes of the business community, the Conservative promised to lower taxes.*

Such sentences begin with a phrase and so withhold their main points (contained in the independent clause) until the end. The technique is effective because, being at the end, the main clause is stressed. Sentences which delay their main clause are called **periodic sentences.**

The order of words in an English sentence is alterable to a considerable degree. Consider:

> *The tenants refused to pay one more penny of rent until the landlord repaired the plumbing.*
> *Until the landlord repaired the plumbing, the tenants refused to pay one more penny of rent.*
> *One more penny of rent the tenants refused to pay, until the landlord repaired the plumbing.*
> *The tenants refused to pay, until the landlord repaired the plumbing, one more penny of rent.*

Which sentence is the most effective? It depends upon the form and shape of the other sentences around it, on the writer's purpose and audience, and on the extent to which the writer wants to emphasise certain information within the sentence. The word order in the third version seems unique and emphatic.

If you notice, when you are revising your work, that the vast majority of your sentences follow the typical subject-verb pattern, consider experimenting with the word order of some of your sentences. There is no 'right' way to determine which version of a sentence is the best. It does help to read your work out loud while you revise it. You will be able to hear the rhythm and flow of your sentences and alter them in order to display them to their best advantage.

Tutorial

Progress questions

Revise each of the following paragraphs to improve their style. Do not alter the meaning of the paragraphs by adding anything to them or taking anything from them. You may rearrange the order and structure of sentences in ways you think most effective.

1. Archimedes was a Greek mathematician. He discovered that the weight of the fluid that was displaced when an object was put in fluid could be used to measure the mass of that object. There is a legend associated with this discovery. Archimedes was in his bath one day. He watched the water rise as he settled into his bath. He realised the weight of an object could be calculated by weighing the amount of fluid it displaced when that object was placed in fluid.

2. Chad is a landlocked country in north-central Africa. Chad is slightly smaller than the state of Alaska. Libya is north of Chad. The Sudan is east of Chad. The Central African

Empire is south of Chad. Cameroon is also south of Chad. Nigeria is southwest of Chad. Niger is west of Chad. Lake Chad is the largest body of water in Chad. It is in the west. It spills into neighbouring Niger and Nigeria. In the north is a desert. It is part of the Sahara Desert.

3 Mercury is the planet nearest the sun. It is named after the Roman messenger to the gods. Mercury was famous for his speed as a runner. It is an appropriate name for the planet. Mercury whizzes around the sun. It travels at the speed of 30 miles per second. It completes one circuit in 88 days. But it rotates slowly on its axis. It takes 59 days for Mercury to make a single rotation. It spins at the rate of about 6 miles per hour. The Earth spins at the rate of about 1,000 miles per hour.

4 In Egyptian mythology Ra is the God of the Sun. He is the supreme god in Egyptian mythology. He was the son of Nut. Nut is the goddess of the heavens. Egyptian pharaohs claimed to be descended from Ra. Ra is sometimes represented as a lion. Ra is sometimes represented as a cat. Ra is sometimes represented as a falcon.

5 When America was founded, the average human life span was 35 years. By 1900, the average life span had increased to 47 years. Today, the average American lives to be 76 years old. An elderly American is defined as one over the age of 65. In 1900, one in 25 Americans was over the age of 65. Today, one in eight Americans is over the age of 65. The explosion in the growth of the number of elderly American has significant social and political ramifications.

6 The land which now comprises the state of Wyoming was purchased in 1803. It was a part of the Louisiana Purchase. Great Britain bought land from France in the Louisiana Purchase. In 1846, the United States obtained Wyoming from the British. The takeover was one of the conditions of the Oregon Treaty.

There are many ways of improving the style of dull and uninspired writing. Here are new versions of paragraphs 1 and 3, which have been revised to improve their style:

1 Archimedes was a Greek mathematician who discovered that the weight of the fluid that was displaced when an object was put in fluid could be used to measure the mass of that object. There is a legend associated with this discovery. Settling into his bath one day, Archimedes watched the water rise. In a flash of insight, he realised that the mass of an object could be calculated by weighing the amount of fluid it displaced when completely immersed.

3 Named after the Roman messenger to the gods, Mercury is the planet nearest the sun. Mercury was famous for his speed as a runner. It is an appropriate name for the planet, as Mercury whizzes around the sun, travelling at a speed of 30 miles per second and completing one circuit in 88 days. It does, however, rotate slowly on its axis. It takes 59 days for Mercury to make a single rotation, spinning at the rate of about 6 miles per hour; this is much slower than the Earth, which spins at the rate of about 1,000 miles per hour.

Discussion points

1 Style is a term we associate not only with writing but also with clothing, architecture, and art. Discuss the parallels between writing style and style as it applies to other creative arts.

2 Compare and contrast the writing styles of one of your favourite writers and one of your friends' favourite writers.

Practical assignment

Find an essay you think is well written. Write a 500-word analysis of the style of this essay. Discuss the author's use of subordination, parallel structure, and periodic sentences.

Study and revision tips

Style is the most sensory of the components of good writing, appealing especially to the senses of sound and sight. As you revise your work, think of ways to make the sound of your words and sentences more pleasing and ways to use imagery effectively to help your reader visualise what it is you are describing.

12 Punctuating Your Sentences Correctly

One-minute overview

Sentences need to be properly punctuated if they are to be clear and readable. An unpunctuated sentence reads like a puzzle which must be solved before its meaning can be grasped. This sentence, for example – 'If you can come before it gets too dark' – is confusing: it reads, in fact, like a sentence fragment. But the meaning becomes clear when a comma is placed after 'can' – 'If you can, come before it gets too dark.' The teachers who will evaluate your writing don't want to solve puzzles. They want to determine that you know your subject and you know how to express that knowledge clearly and effectively. Part of clear and effective expression is the correct use of punctuation marks. It is important that you know the correct punctuation marks to use:

- at the end of a sentence
- within sentences
- within words.

Punctuation at the end of a sentence

At the end of most declarative, informative sentences you will use a **full stop**. You may use an **exclamation mark** (!) for extra emphasis, but, in an academic essay, do so sparingly. A **question mark**, of course, comes at the end of a question.

It is acceptable to use a **semi-colon** at the end of a sentence, if the next sentence continues on the same topic:

American Motors manufactures fewer than half a million passenger cars a year; Ford Motors manufactures well over a million.
The Asian economy faltered in the late 1990s; lately it has shown signs of a recovery.

A full stop would be acceptable between these sentences, but the semi-colon does emphasise the relationship between them. A comma would not be acceptable. A comma cannot come between two complete sentences unless the comma is followed by a coordinate conjunction (see Chapter 9).

It is acceptable to use a **colon** at the end of a sentence, if the next sentence explains or clarifies a topic mentioned in the original sentence:

He realised, with great sorrow, that there was no other choice: he would have to fight his own brother.
In the course of the lecture, he explained to us that the city's name derives from the native language: 'hono' means 'bay' and 'lulu' means 'sheltered'.

A full stop would be acceptable between these sentences, but the colon does stress the fact that the second sentence embellishes the first.

Punctuation within a sentence

There are six punctuation marks that can occur within a sentence. They are the comma, the semi-colon, the colon, the dash, quotation marks, and the ellipsis.

The comma

There are four main rules which govern the use of commas in academic writing.

1. A comma comes **before a coordinate conjunction** in a compound sentence. Here is an example:

   The topic sentence should contain the main ideas of the paragraph, and the other sentences should develop the main idea.

   Note that this rule is also covered in Chapter 9, under the sub-heading 'The Run-on Sentence.'

2. Commas **separate a non-restrictive** word, phrase, or clause from the rest of the sentence. A non-restrictive element is one that is not essential to the meaning of the sentence. It is the opposite of a restricted element, which is essential to the meaning of the sentence. Consider carefully these two sentences:

   Sheehy's Guide to Reference Books, which should be at the reference desk of your library, will list sources that will be useful to you.

   All of the books that I need to research my essay have been signed out of the library.

   Note that the clause 'which should be at the reference desk of your library' is separated from the rest of the sentence by commas. Commas are used because the clause is non-restrictive, is not essential to the meaning of the sentence. Eliminate the clause and the sentence still makes sense:

   Sheehy's Guide to Reference Books will list sources that will be useful to you.

   Now note the clause 'that I need to research my essay' in the second sentence. This clause is not separated from the rest of the sentence by commas. It is a restrictive clause. It is essential to the meaning of the sentence. Eliminate this clause from the sentence and the sentence no longer makes sense:

   All of the books have been signed out of the library.

If you can eliminate a word, phrase, or clause from a sentence, and if the sentence is still logical after you have eliminated the word, phrase, or clause, then that word, phrase, or clause is non-restrictive and should be separated from the rest of the sentence by commas.

Consider this sentence:

Windsor Castle was damaged by a serious fire.

This sentence is short, simple, and self-contained. Any clauses or phrases that might be added to this sentence would be non-restrictive and therefore separated from the rest of the sentence by commas. Note carefully the commas in this sentence:

In 1992, Windsor Castle, the Queen's house on the banks of the Thames, was damaged by a serious fire.

Transitional and parenthetical words and phrases are almost always non-restrictive and are, therefore, set off from the rest of the sentence by commas. Note carefully the placement of commas in these sentences. They separate transitional and parenthetical words and phrases off from the rest of the sentence:

> *There is, however, no reason why a new policy cannot be implemented immediately.*
>
> *Finally, we are considering the implementation of a new policy which should reduce the rate of recidivism.*
>
> *On the other hand, the current policy has reduced the crime rate in some sections of the city.*
>
> *That, too, remains to be decided.*

There is an **exception** to the rule which states that restrictive words, phrases, or clauses are not set off from the rest of the sentence with commas: even a restrictive word phrase or clause will usually be followed by a comma, if that restrictive element begins the sentence. Compare these two sentences:

> *Their starting point guard will not be able to play unless her Achilles tendon is better.*
>
> *Unless her Achilles tendon is better, their starting point guard will not be able to play.*

3. Use a comma **between coordinate but not cumulative adjectives.** Coordinate adjectives modify the same noun. In the phrase 'a bright, colourful skirt' both adjectives modify the noun 'skirt' and are separated from each other by a comma. A cumulative adjective qualifies the adjective which follows it; that adjective modifies the noun. In the phrase 'a black leather skirt' the adjective 'black' qualifies the adjective 'leather' which then modifies the noun 'skirt'. These are cumulative adjectives and are not separated from each other by commas. An often-used test to determine if adjectives are coordinate or cumulative is to see if the word 'and' can be placed between the adjectives. If it can, the adjectives are coordinate and need a comma between them: a bright and colourful skirt. If 'and' sounds awkward placed between the adjectives, a comma is not required: 'She wore a black and leather skirt.'

4. Use commas to separate words, phrases, or clauses **in a series**. Note the use of the commas in this sentence:

> *In this chapter, we are learning the uses of the full stop, the comma, the semi-colon, the colon, and the dash.*

Commas separate the series of punctuation marks mentioned in the sentence. Note that there is a comma between the words 'colon' and 'dash'. This comma is optional. Note, as well, the comma after the introductory phrase 'In this chapter'. It is a non-restrictive phrase and is therefore set off from the rest of the sentence by the comma.

The semi-colon

There are two uses for the semi-colon in academic writing.

1. Use a semi-colon **to separate two complete but related sentences.**

> *On one side of the street were protesters who wanted the child returned to his father in Cuba; on the other side were protesters who insisted the child be allowed to stay in the country.*
>
> *The schools in the cabinet minister's riding all have access to the Internet; inner city schools do not have even basic computer equipment.*

2. Use a semi-colon **to separate phrases or clauses in a series** when there are commas within those phrases or clauses. In the following sentence, two of the 'you want' clauses contain commas, which is why the clauses are separated from each other by semi-colons:

> *You want your essay to be well organised; you want your sentences within your paragraphs and your paragraphs with the essay to be logically connected, in other words, to cohere; you want your diction to be accurate and appropriate; you want to avoid errors in grammar, spelling, and punctuation; and you want your prose to be concise.*

The colon

Earlier in this chapter, you learned that a colon could come between two sentences if the second sentence explained or clarified the first – 'He adhered to the golden rule: Do unto others as you would have others do unto you.'

A colon also **precedes a word or a phrase that explains or clarifies a sentence**:

> *Brighton is a long way away: 184 kilometres, to be exact.*

Note that the clarifying word(s) or phrase often takes the form of a list:

> *She claimed there were just three qualities she was looking for in a husband: ambition, compassion, and a good sense of humour.*

Note also that the clarifying word or phrase can come before the complete sentence. If this is the case, that clarifying word group is followed by the colon:

> *Joe Average: that was the appropriate pseudonym he chose for himself.*

Quotation marks

In academic writing, quotation marks serve two functions.

1. Quotation marks indicate that you are **quoting someone else's spoken or written words**.

   > *'I write slowly,' Mullen told one interviewer. 'It can take me months to complete a single sonnet.'*
   >
   > *In her preface to Satan's Rainbow, Mullen responds to criticism that her work is obscure, arguing that her ambiguous syntax is a 'deliberate strategy to free readers to interpret my work in ways that mean the most to them' (xix).*

   Note that if a written quote is more than about three lines in length, it is set off and from the rest of the text and would not contain quotation marks (unless the source being quoted also contained them).

   Note also that, on occasion, you might need to use quotation marks in a context in which other quotation marks already occur. When this happens, revert to double quotation marks to indicate the quote within the quote:

> *In her analysis of Keats's sonnet, Foster notes that 'the repetition of the adverb "still" is typical of Keats's style'.*

2. Quotation marks enclose **minor titles**. Titles of short stories and poems, for example, are placed within quotation marks: My favourite sonnet is 'Bright Star' by Keats.

The dash

In academic writing, the dash is used mainly to enclose a non-restrictive word group that contains commas:

> *She eats something from each food group – protein, dairy, fruits and vegetables, and grains – at every meal.*

A dash is also used to signal an abrupt change or shift in thought, but a sentence that contains such a shift would be rare in academic writing:

> *Student can also pay for a database search – if they want to waste their time and money.*

Parentheses

Parentheses enclose information of borderline importance to a sentence, in other words, information which a writer decides to include but does not consider vitally important:

> *The first volume (in a 12-volume series) should be published before the end of the month.*

Ellipsis

The ellipsis mark (a succession of three full stops) is an important punctuation mark in academic writing, used to indicate that unneeded words have been omitted. The ellipsis comes in handy if you are quoting from a secondary source, and you want to keep the quote concise and relevant by omitting unnecessary words:

> *Computer viruses are more annoying than harmful and most hackers cannot do anywhere near the damage... they claim they can.*

Use four dots if a full stop is included in the information you omit.

Punctuation within a word

There are two punctuation marks that can occur within a word. They are the apostrophe and the hyphen.

The apostrophe

Apostrophes are used in nouns to indicate ownership. Study carefully the following sentences:

> *The tutor claimed he had misplaced his student's essay.*
>
> *The tutor claimed he had misplaced his students' essays.*
>
> *For that assignment, the men's essays were not as well written as the women's.*

In the first sentence, the apostrophe comes before the 's' because the noun 'student' is singular. There is only one student. In the second sentence, the apostrophe comes after the 's' because the noun 'students' is plural.

The rule, then, is **put an apostrophe before the 's' to indicate singular possession, and after the 's' to indicate plural possession.**

What about the third sentence? Men and women are plural: why does the apostrophe come before the 's'? It comes before the 's' because 'men' and 'women' are nouns that form their plural not by adding an 's' but by changing a vowel: 'man' becomes 'men'; 'woman', 'women'.

The apostrophe comes before the 's' in nouns that form their plural by changing a vowel. We write children's toys, never childrens' toys.

If a noun ends in the letter 's', you may put the apostrophe after the 's' and not add another 's' even if the noun is singular: 'I enjoy reading Keats' poetry'; 'I enjoy reading Keats's poetry.' Choose the version that sounds the best to you.

Apostrophes are also used in contractions: 'don't', 'isn't', etc. But note carefully the difference between **it's** and **its.** 'It's' is a contraction for 'it is'. Its is a possessive pronoun and never needs an apostrophe because it is already in possessive case. Memorise this sentence to avoid confusing the two: It's missing one of its pages.

Finally, note the placement of the apostrophe in these sentences:

We are having dinner at Mary and Tom's house.
I wrecked my brother-in-law's car.

The hyphen

Hyphens are used within compound words: 'mother-in-law', 'forty-one', 'one-third'.

Hyphens are used to join two or more words which modify a noun they precede: 'She wore five-inch heels.'

Tutorial

Progress questions

Punctuate the following sentences correctly. Correct errors that presently appear in some of the sentences. Some sentences are already correctly punctuated.

1. We planned to serve key lime pie but my brother is allergic to citrus fruit.
2. Oscar will be fighting an inexperienced opponent and experts are predicting an early knockout.
3. Your essay should be double spaced and should have one and a half inch margins on both sides of the page.
4. My uncle who played basketball in college taught me how to dribble behind my back.
5. She decided to retire early, she could not handle the stress any longer.
6. Both a coordinate conjunction and a conjunctive adverb link sentences together, a conjunctive adverb is preceded by a semicolon.
7. The schools in the minister's riding now have access to the Internet, however inner-city schools are still waiting to get basic computer equipment.
8. Ellis did not hand in two of his assignments, therefore he did not get a passing grade in his sociology course.
9. Tia Maria Drambuie Benedictine and Curacao are among the most popular liqueurs and are sold throughout the world.
10. The tern is a slender gull like bird and with it's long pointed wings and a deeply notched tail it flies with grace energy and strength.
11. The silver that is mined in Mexico is considered superior to the silver mined in Colorado.
12. The upper limit of the biosphere the part of earth where life can exist is about 9000 metres above sea level the lower

limit is approximately 3000 metres beneath the surface of the ocean.

13 A portion of the play the third scene of the final act to be precise was excluded to meet two hour time limit.

14 The anteaters tongue is covered with sticky saliva which allows it to trap ants termites and other insects on which it feeds.

15 Daves new interest is cybernetics the science that among other things compares brain functions to the function of machines especially computers.

16 France lost Alsace and Lorraine to Germany in 1871 after a war in which the Germans who were better prepared than the French won nearly every battle.

17 The greyhound wolfhound and deerhound hunt by sight the bloodhound foxhound and beagle hunt by scent.

18 Diabetics lack insulin which controls the supply of sugar from the blood to the muscles however with proper insulin injections diabetics can live a normal life.

19 Film adaptations of novels are usually disappointing but the film version of Kinsellas Field of Dreams is better than the book.

20 Since the beginning of the century the Nobel Prize has been awarded to men and women for outstanding contributions to the following fields physics chemistry medicine literature peace and economics.

21 AsT. S. Eliot writes in Little Gidding one of the poems from his book Four QuartetsWhat we call the beginning is often the end And to make an end is to make a beginning.

22 Originally the word tycoon from the Japanese taikun referred to the commander in chief of the Japanese army but now its used often in a derogatory sense to describe a powerful influential businessperson.

23 The plane will make a ninety minute stop in St. Louis where you are free to disembark for thirty minutes a twenty minute stop in Minneapolis where you many not disembark

and another ninety minute stop in Montreal whey again you may disembark for twenty minutes.

24 Steroids enhance athletic performance but to quote professor W.S. Benson the short term gain in strength is not worth the long term health risks to which a steroid user exposes himself.

Here are the corrected versions of the above sentences.

1 We planned to serve key lime pie, but my brother is allergic to citrus fruit.

2 Oscar will be fighting an inexperienced opponent, and experts are predicting an early knockout.

3 Your essay should be double-spaced and should have 1.5 inch margins on both sides of the page.

4 My uncle, who played basketball in college, taught me how to dribble behind my back.

5 She decided to retire early; she could not handle the stress any longer.

6 Both a coordinate conjunction and a conjunctive adverb link sentences together, but a conjunctive adverb is preceded by a semicolon.

7 The schools in the minister's riding now have access to the Internet; however, inner-city schools are still waiting to get basic computer equipment.

8 Ellis did not hand in two of his assignments; therefore he did not get a passing grade in his sociology course.

9 Tia Maria, Drambuie, Benedictine and Curacao are among the most popular liqueurs and are sold throughout the world.

10 The tern is a slender gull-like bird and, with its long pointed wings and a deeply notched tail, it flies with grace, energy and strength.

11 The silver that is mined in Mexico is considered superior to the silver mined in Colorado.

12 The upper limit of the biosphere, the part of earth where life

can exist, is about 9,000 metres above sea level; the lower limit is approximately 3,000 metres beneath the surface of the ocean.

13 A portion of the play – the third scene of the final act, to be precise – was excluded to meet the two-hour time limit.

14 The anteater's tongue is covered with sticky saliva, which allows it to trap ants, termites and other insects on which it feeds.

15 Dave's new interest is cybernetics, the science that, among other things, compares brain functions to the function of machines, especially computers.

16 France lost Alsace and Lorraine to Germany in 1871, after a war in which the Germans, who were better prepared than the French, won nearly every battle.

17 The greyhound, wolfhound and deerhound hunt by sight; the bloodhound, foxhound and beagle hunt by scent.

18 Diabetics lack insulin, which controls the supply of sugar from the blood to the muscles; however, with proper insulin injections diabetics can live a normal life.

19 Film adaptations of novels are usually disappointing, but the film version of Kinsella's *Field of Dreams* is better than the book.

20 Since the beginning of the century the Nobel Prize has been awarded to men and women for outstanding contributions to the following fields: physics, chemistry, medicine, literature, peace and economics.

21 As T.S. Eliot writes in 'Little Gidding,' one of the poems from his book *Four Quartets*, 'What we call the beginning is often the end /And to make an end is to make a beginning.'

22 Originally the word 'tycoon' from the Japanese *taikun* referred to the commander-in-chief of the Japanese army, but now it's often used in a derogatory sense to describe a powerful, influential businessperson.

23 The plane will make a 90-minute stop in St. Louis, where you are free to disembark for 30 minutes; a 20-minute stop

in Minneapolis, where you many not disembark; and another 90-minute stop in Montreal, where, again, you may disembark for 20 minutes.

24 Steroids enhance athletic performance but, to quote Professor W.S. Benson, 'the short-term gain in strength is not worth the long-term health risks to which a steroid user exposes himself'.

Discussion points

1. Discuss how and why proper punctuation contributes to the clarity of writing.
2. Discuss some rhetorical circumstances under which certain punctuation marks are interchangeable.

Practical assignments

In an essay of approximately 500 words, compare and contrast the use of the colon and the use of the semi-colon.

The use of a comma in an English sentence is sometimes quite arbitrary. Describe and discuss three comma rules which writers may disobey under certain circumstances. Don't forget to provide examples.

Study and revision tip

There are many rules that govern the punctuation of English sentences. When you are working on a writing assignment, have a guide to writing (such as this one) close by to consult when you are uncertain about how one of your sentences should be punctuated.

13

Choosing the Best Words

One-minute overview

The word is the smallest unit of written communication but by no means any less important than the sentence or the paragraph. In academic writing, you have to take as much care selecting appropriate words as you do in structuring sentences and paragraphs. Use words appropriate to the **context** of your essay; use words that best convey the **meaning** you wish to convey; and use words that convey the **tone** and the **voice** that are appropriate for academic writing.

Establishing context

The words you choose must be appropriate to the context in which you use them. Academic writing is relatively formal, so the **connotation** of your words as well as the **denotation** must be accurate. The denotation of a word is the word's literal, dictionary definition. The connotation refers to the intellectual or emotional associations a word carries with it. Words can have identical denotations. A six-foot-tall 130-pound man can be described as 'skinny' or 'slender' but would rather be 'slender' because the connotations of that word are more positive.

Slang words usually have connotations too informal for academic writing. In this sentence, some verbs would be acceptable in academic writing, some would not: 'The MP was (drunk, inebriated, intoxicated, blitzed, bombed, tipsy, pissed to the gills, shitfaced, wasted, looped, swacked).'

The use of **jargon** also depends upon context. Jargon is language specific to a certain social or professional group. Lawyers, stockbrokers, doctors, basketball, football, and baseball aficionados, computer programmers, forest rangers, civil servants, and trumpet, piano, and violin players can all speak and write in a language they understand but outsiders do not. Readers can usually identify the social or professional group using the jargon but not the meaning of all of the words and phrases they use. Try to identify the social or professional group responsible for the jargon in these sentences and try to 'translate' these sentences into jargon-free English:

It has side rocker panels, flared wheel wells, and an inline six cylinder, 2.5-litre 168-horsepower engine.
O'Neal took it to the hole for a slam but Smits was called for three in the paint so the bucket didn't count.
By cutting on the bias, she accentuated the drape on the handkerchief hems she will show in next spring's collection.

The use of jargon is not necessarily an error. Its appropriateness depends upon the writer's knowledge of her audience. If the writer knows her readers will understand the jargon because they are members of the apposite subculture, she may use that subculture's jargon. But if her readers are not a part of that subculture, the writer must avoid its jargon and use layman's language or else readers will have trouble understanding the text and may even resent the writer who is making them feel like outsiders.

Determining the meaning

Always **choose the specific and concrete word** over the vague and abstract one. Concrete and specific words add important shades of meaning to the sentences in which they appear. Compare, for example, these two sentences:

Eric was at the bus stop when a car sped past him, hit the puddle, and splashed water over his new suit.
Eric was at the bus stop when a Mercedes sped past him, hit the puddle, and splashed water over his new suit.

Only one word has been changed: 'car' has become 'Mercedes'. But the effect of the change is considerable. The reader now sees more vividly what the writer is trying to describe. And Eric's anger has an additional cause. Mercedes suggests wealth, which, in turn, suggests indifference to poor people waiting for buses. The Mercedes adds insult to the injury. The Mercedes makes an indifferent sentence considerably more interesting.

Your meaning will also be enhanced if you use **euphemisms** discreetly. A euphemism is a word or a phrase which, at best, is deliberately obscure and, at worst, is deliberately deceptive. There are two reasons for using a euphemism.

Euphemisms are sometimes used to avoid being too blunt or offensive. A teacher might like to write on a report card: 'Arthur is loud and obnoxious. He annoys me and the other children in the class. We can't get any work done when he is around, so I often send him to the quiet room where he has to do his work alone.' But, unwilling to risk the ire of parents and headteachers, she will more likely resort to euphemism: 'We appreciate Arthur's exuberant personality, though it does interfere sometimes with class work. I encourage Arthur to work independently, which he seems to enjoy.'

But sometimes euphemisms are used to deflect the truth, to mislead readers deliberately. Management cannot let the plant close, so an accident becomes a 'reportable occurrence', which sounds much less threatening. The military can't admit it erred, so civilians killed in the bombing raids are referred to as 'collateral damage', which sounds like an unfortunate but inevitable and harmless by-product of war. The government 'initiates revenue enhancement programmes' so we don't quite realise our taxes are going to go up. This type of euphemism does not, like the type discussed earlier, avoid offending readers. It obfuscates and misleads and should, therefore, be avoided.

Choosing the right voice

Written discourse reflects the personality and the attitude of the writer, or at least the personality and the attitude the writer has chosen to assume for a given assignment. This personality and attitude is known as the writer's **voice.** Writers must assume a voice that complements the purpose of their work, the audience for whom it is intended, and the genre in which it is written.

A movie reviewer might choose to use a sardonic voice to pan a film: 'Curiously, her performance, as lame as it is, complements the plot which is every bit as superficial.' Valedictorians typically assume a solemn, rather formal voice: 'We will leave here today to continue along the road of life and conquer the challenges that await us, but we will pause sometimes to remember Madison High, the teachers who not only taught us but nurtured us, the friends who brightened the good times and helped us through the bad.' You will likely choose an informal voice in an email to a friend: 'Hot gossip, girlfriend: E. and L. are over. Word is Eric drove past Scott's place and saw Linda's car in the driveway. Naturally he freaked...'

Our concern here, of course, is with **academic voice**, the persona writers assume when writing an essay for a tutor or an article for a professional journal. A good academic voice is formal but not too lofty or grandiose. Academic voice is clear and concise. Most of your textbooks are written in academic voice. Academic voice is more formal than informal but accessible to its audience.

The point of view of academic voice is a topic of some debate. Some of your tutors will not want you to use the first person pronoun (I) and will not want you to address your readers in second person, that is, as 'you'. Others won't mind. There are precedents for both. The use of first-person and second-person pronouns is common in some textbooks and journal articles and avoided in others.

Academic voice does not presuppose the use of **ostentatious language**, that is words and phrases which are used not because they are the most appropriate but because they are the most complex and obscure. Writers who use ostentatious language are merely trying to impress their readers with their extensive and sophisticated vocabulary. But readers usually suspect the truth: that the writer has consulted his thesaurus one too many times. Good writers eschew obfuscation with unambiguous linguistic manifestations.

An example

Let's look at an example of good academic writing and examine its diction and voice more closely. It is from *Writing Your Master's Thesis*, edited by Alan Bond, published by Studymates, page 25. The author is discussing the uses of two types of qualitative data for a research study, the questionnaire and the interview.

> *The questionnaire is often used to generate quantitative data but it can also act as a means of uncovering more qualitative information. In either case it will be used to survey a relatively large number of respondents with very specific questions. Even where qualitative data are sought, these will often be analysed in a quantitative manner. You could for instance use a questionnaire to determine the attitudes of the residents of a village to a new bypass. You could ask them to grade their views about the bypass, from very necessary to totally unnecessary, and then quantify the results. In this way, attitudinal data which is qualitative can be analysed and presented in a quantitative manner. The purpose of the questionnaire is usually to undertake extensive research, seeing broad patterns of thought and behaviour within a sample population.*
>
> *Other types of qualitative data do not lend themselves to quantification, since they concern the views and beliefs of individuals or small groups. The purpose is not to discover how*

many people share the same attitude (as with a questionnaire) but to uncover the meanings and intentions of specific actors in specific situations. In this instance, interviews will normally be used rather than questionnaires, since these offer a good means of examining experiences, feelings and values. You could, for instance, use interviews to find out from transport officials why they decided to build the bypass around that particular village, or you could interview road protesters about why they were trying to prevent the bypass from being built. In either case an interview would be an appropriate way of constructing the relevant data.

Note that the diction here is formal but not pedantic. The author does not sound like a supercilious professor, as he might had he tried to be too formal and written: 'You could, for instance, dialogue with transport officials as to why they decided to construct the bypass around that particular rural community, or you could interview road dissenters about why they were trying to avert the bypass from its imminent construction.' Nor does he sound obtuse, as he might had he opted for an informal style and written: 'Rap with a few transport officials and get to why they're screwing up this town with their ugly-ass bypass or chat up the...' Instead, he writes: 'You could, for instance, use interviews to find out from transport officials why they decided to build the bypass around that particular village, or you could interview road protesters about why they were trying to prevent the bypass from being built.' His tone is measured, his diction neither sends the reader to her dictionary nor insults her intelligence. The passage is not without jargon – '...attitudinal data which is qualitative...' – but the author, rightly, presupposes a reader with some knowledge of research protocol and so uses jargon appropriately. The words are specific and concrete, appropriate in their connotations, academic but not ostentatious and reflect the voice of a learned man educating his readers about a topic of importance to them.

Our case study continued

Having revised her essay, Audrey focuses on the final phase of the writing process, the editing. Writers proofread and edit their work as they draft and revise – as, indeed, Audrey has done. But good writers also take the time to proofread carefully one last time, looking exclusively for editing errors. Often, they will use an editing checklist of some kind at this final stage in the process, to guide them and remind them what needs to be checked. Here is the checklist Audrey used:

Editing checklist

- My essay has cohesive ties, clarifying relationships between and among sentences and paragraphs.
- The tone and voice of my writing are appropriate for an academic essay.
- There is a rhythm and flow to my writing, a blend of sentence types.
- I have checked for and corrected errors in sentence structure (run-on sentences, sentence fragments).
- I have checked for and corrected errors in sentence grammar (pronoun case and reference, subject–verb agreement, verb tense).
- I have checked for and corrected errors in spelling.
- I have checked for and corrected errors in punctuation.

Audrey must still double check her sources and make certain her reference list is complete and accurate. But, other than that, she has finished. She has reflected upon her topic, done her research, planned, drafted, revised and edited. She has produced the following solid effort.

Audrey's Essay

Audrey B. Fisher
English 270
Professor Fareed
February, 2005

Prototypes for the Characters in Shakespeare's Sonnets

William Shakespeare was a master at describing and developing characters who are so complex and intriguing that they have become a part of our shared cultural heritage. Most literate people in the English-speaking world, indeed the whole world, know of Lear, Othello, Falstaff, Hamlet, Shylock, Macbeth, Romeo and Juliet. Many of Shakespeare's characters seem so real, in part, because they were based upon historical figures, even if the playwright did use some dramatic licence in depicting these people, their motives and their actions. Similarly, the people who appear in Shakespeare's famous sequence of 154 sonnets are rendered so authentic that many scholars, encouraged by Shakespeare's tendency to base his characters on real people, have suggested that, taken together, the sonnets tell a story based on the poet's own experiences and that the characters in the sonnets have real-life prototypes.

Here is the story the sonnets seem to tell. In late 16th-century London there was a rich and cultured nobleman – a patron, supporter and friend of the best poets and playwrights. Among these poets and playwrights was William Shakespeare, who, in a sequence of sonnets, sings the praises of this nobleman, stressing his generosity, striking good looks, and refined taste. In some of the sonnets he urges his friend to marry – apparently he was reluctant to do so – in order to have children, both to perpetuate his superior gene pool and to ensure his immortality. The poems tell the friend how important he is in the poet's life and how the friendship brightens the spirits of the poet whenever he is feeling down:

For thy sweet love remembered such wealth brings
That then I scorn to change my state with kings.
(29. 13–14)

The friend is the patron of another poet, whom Shakespeare considers a rival and of whom he is therefore rather jealous. Even more disturbing, this friend and patron becomes entranced by a free-spirited dark lady who happens to be Shakespeare's own mistress. In the later sonnets, the poet tells of his suspicion that his best friend and his dark lady are lovers. The sonnets express Shakespeare's concern and agitation, as he tries to cope with the duplicity of his two best friends (Hecht 15). But, in the end, he forgives his friend and even apologises for his own infidelity.

Who were these people? Who was the nobleman who sponsored and befriended the poet? Who was the rival poet who also, to the poet's dismay, had the support of this wealthy benefactor? Who was the beautiful, mysterious dark lady who became first the author's and then the nobleman's mistress? Were they real people or merely the products of Shakespeare's incomparable imagination?

The patron/friend is featured in sonnets 1–126, the bulk of Shakespeare's collection. The poet describes him as a handsome, indeed beautiful young man, extremely intelligent and refined. This description fits Henry Wriothesley, the Earl of Southampton, and many Shakespeare scholars believe Southampton is the friend featured in many of the sonnets. Southampton was 20 in 1593, when Shakespeare was probably working on his sonnets (Hubler 12). He was a nobleman and a patron of the arts. Shakespeare explicitly dedicates some of his other poems to Southampton, in a way that suggests they were close friends (Hubler 12). But there is a problem with confirming the identity of Henry Wriothesley as the sonnets' protagonist. The sonnets are dedicated to their 'ONLIE BEGETTER,' whom most experts believe to be the person who inspired the sonnets, in other words the special friend (Sorenson). In the dedication, this friend is identified by his initials. The initials are 'W.H.', which reverses those of Henry

Wriothesley. Either the printer made a mistake, the author was being deliberately coy and partially hiding his benefactor's identity or the Earl of Southampton was not the special friend of the sonnets.

Another contender, one who has the right initials, is William Herbert, the third earl of Pembroke. Herbert, like Wriothesley, was a handsome and intelligent nobleman and a patron of poets and playwrights. The editors of the 1623 collection of Shakespeare's plays dedicated the volume to Herbert and his brother in a way that suggests Shakespeare knew the young earl quite well (Hubler 13). Dover Wilson makes a strong case in Pembroke's favour by pointing out parallels between the content of the sonnets and Pembroke's life, especially in the on-again-off-again negotiations for his marriage, hinted at in sonnets 1–17 (xcvi–ci), and by noting the frequency with which the poet puns on the name 'Will' in reference to the friend. But although the initials are right, a problem remains. Herbert was barely a teenager when most experts – Wilson is an exception – agree the sonnets were written. One of the sonnets does refer to the friend as a 'fair boy'. But the sonnets clearly celebrate the friendship and the personal qualities of a young man, not a young adolescent.

A.L. Rowse believes that W.H. is William Harvey. He believes that 'begetter' refers not to the friend who inspired the sonnets but to the man who literally delivered the sonnets to the publisher, Thomas Thorpe. Harvey was the third husband of the Countess of Southampton, who also happened to be the mother of Henry Wriothesley. She died in 1607 and left her estate to Harvey. Rowse believes that the estate included the manuscript of the sonnets and that Harvey passed them to Thorpe who published them in 1609 (Rowse xi). Rowse believes that the friend featured in the first 126 sonnets is Henry Wriothesley, the Earl of Southampton, but that it was William Harvey who was the sonnets' 'begetter'.

In Sonnet 79, a new character appears on the scene. He is a rival poet who makes Shakespeare jealous because he, too, receives patronage from W.H. He is difficult to identify because there were so many poets in Elizabethan England, and most of them sought the patronage of a nobleman. Shakespeare describes his rival's poetic style in ways that suggest, to most experts, the work of Samuel Daniel or George Chapman, both of whom wrote sonnet collections (Hubler 18–19). John Dover Wilson makes a strong case for Chapman by explicating Sonnet 86 and seeing within it echoes of Chapman's own work, which Shakespeare mocks (lxix).

Rowse's choice is the second best poet of the age, Christopher Marlowe. Marlowe was openly gay, and Wriothesley was probably bisexual. Rowse's implication is that there was a sexual empathy, if not a relationship, between the two, which the heterosexual Shakespeare could not handle. (There has been much speculation about Shakespeare's sexuality, as revealed in the sonnets, but he does indicate, in Sonnet 20, that his own relationship with this friend is non-sexual.) The rival poet disappears from the sonnets at about the halfway point in a way that suggests, if the order of the sonnets is chronological, that Shakespeare won the battle for the patron's generosity. This lends some credence to Rowse's belief that Marlowe is the rival. Rowse suggests that Shakespeare's victory was due not to his superior ability but to tragic circumstance. Marlowe was killed in a bar-room brawl in 1593, the time most experts believe Shakespeare was working on his sonnet collection (Rowse xviii). After Marlowe's death, Shakespeare had no rival; hence, the rival poet disappears as a character.

The existence of the dark lady is hinted at in earlier sonnets, but she does not really emerge as a fully fledged character until Sonnet 127. She is a beautiful, dark-haired woman who becomes the narrator's mistress. But she is unfaithful to the narrator and her infidelity torments him. He suspects that one of her lovers is the patron/friend, and the tone of those sonnets in which he speculates about the double deception reflects the torment of a man unable to deal with the possibility that his two closest friends are deceiving him. In Sonnet 144, he gives voice to his anxiety:

Two loves I have of comfort and despair,
Which like two spirits do suggest me still:

...

To win me soon to hell, my female evil
Tempteth my better angel from my side...
(1–2; 5–6)

If Wriothesley is the patron/friend, then Elizabeth Vernon could be the infamous dark lady (Hubler 17). Vernon was a lady-in-waiting to Queen Elizabeth I. As an earl, Wriothesley was regularly at court and, although the Queen expected him to marry another and actually imprisoned him because of his liaison with Vernon, the two nevertheless married in May of 1598. The sonnets were probably written five years before this, so if Shakespeare and Southampton were indeed competing for the affections of Vernon, Southampton won. The Wriothesleys had a daughter four months after they married (Hubler 17).

If William Herbert is the patron/friend, then the dark lady could be Mary Fitton who, like Vernon, worked for the Queen. Pembroke and Fitton never married but they did have a son together in 1601 (Hubler 17). However, dates militate against the identity of Fitton as the dark lady and against Pembroke as the friend. The sonnets would have had to have been written later than the early 1590s, which most experts believe is possible but unlikely. Moreover a portrait, apparently of Fitton, shows her to have a fair complexion (Wilson lix).

Rowse believes that the dark lady is Emilia Lanier. She was the daughter of one of the Queen's court musicians, but was orphaned as a child and raised by the Countess of Kent (xx). She was intelligent and talented. She inherited her father's musical ability – the dark lady does play the virginal – and she published a long and accomplished poem in 1611. She was married to Alphonse Lanier, another musician employed by Elizabeth. Emilia was apparently the mistress of Lord Hunsdon who was, as the Lord Chamberlain, a patron of Shakespeare's theatre company, so William and Emilia probably knew each other. But Rowse presents no hard evidence that Emilia knew Shakespeare, let alone had a love affair with him. He makes much of puns on Lanier's first name, which he mistakenly claims is William (Hunt 372). Rowse believes Wriothesley is the patron/friend, so if Emilia is the dark lady the two of them must have had a sexual relationship. According to Rowse's interpretation of the sonnets, Shakespeare, almost 30, became infatuated with Emilia the 24-year-old wife of a court musician. They became lovers but soon Emilia (clearly sexually liberated) tired of the playwright and became intimate with the Earl of Southampton, who was a friend of her husband (Rowse xx). Rowse's version of the events is fascinating but his evidence is very circumstantial.

Some scholars believe it is fruitless, even irresponsible, to try to match the sonnet characters to any real people. Stephen Booth, for example, in an otherwise exhaustive analysis of the sonnets, dismisses efforts to uncover the identity of the dark lady, calling such attempts 'wanton and ludicrous' (549) and refusing to speculate himself. Others argue that it is futile to examine the life of Shakespeare to establish the identity of the characters because someone else – maybe Francis Bacon, maybe the Earl of Oxford – is the true author of the sonnets (Hollander). Katharine Wilson suggests that the sonnets are entirely fictitious, in fact a parody of the sonnet genre that was so popular in late 16th-century Europe. Wilson suggests that by addressing the sonnets to a man and to a lascivious dark-skinned woman, instead of to the usual chaste blonde, Shakespeare is satirising the whole sonnet genre. She compares individual Shakespeare sonnets to the sonnets of a variety of contemporary poets to illustrate exactly how Shakespeare parodies specific poems.

But readers, especially modern readers so exposed to the gossip of tabloids and television, will continue to read the sonnets as autobiographical. A story of sex, deception and jealousy, set amidst the highest social and artistic circles, is bound to arouse interest and cause speculation about the identity of the people who figure in the story. Unless there is a major historical discovery, we will never know who these people truly were, if they were, indeed, real. But Shakespeare scholars will continue to speculate about the identity of W.H., the dark lady, and the rival poet – three people who may have figured very prominently in the life of the greatest of all English poets.

Tutorial

Progress questions

Compose five sentences, each of which contains an example of one of the diction errors covered in this chapter:

- inappropriate connotation
- jargon
- vague/abstract language
- euphemism
- ostentatious language.

Then write a revised version of each sentence in which you correct the diction errors.

Discussion points

1. Why do cultures cultivate their own jargon?
2. When are euphemisms acceptable? When are they unacceptable?

Practical assignment

Write an essay of approximately 500 words which presents an extended definition of one of the following terms: jargon, euphemism, connotation. Don't forget to provide specific examples.

Study and revision tips

Use your thesaurus but use it discriminately.

Mark Twain once said that the difference between the right word and the nearly-right word is the difference between lightning and a lightning bug.

14 Acknowledging Sources Accurately and Completely

One-minute overview

You learned in Chapter 2 how to access and use books, the Internet, and articles in scholarly journals to gather some of the information you will need to incorporate into your academic essays in order to make them detailed and authoritative. It is essential that you acknowledge these sources. If you do not acknowledge, accurately and completely, the information you took from sources and incorporated into your essay, you could be guilty of plagiarism. Plagiarism is a form of fraud, in which a writer uses another's words or ideas or knowledge without acknowledgement. It is considered to be a serious offence within academic communities and, in extreme cases, may be punishable by expulsion.

Unfortunately, there is not a single, universally recognised and accepted method of acknowledging secondary sources within the text of an academic essay. There are several different methods and even within sanctioned methods there can be minor differences. But there are two widely-used methods, one of which will be acceptable to most of the teachers for whom you write academic essays. Most of your teachers will accept either:

- footnotes within the text of your essay, or
- a source list at the end of your essay.

Footnotes

The footnote[1] system is relatively straightforward. Whenever a writer has borrowed information from a secondary source or quotes directly from a secondary source, he or she places a number in superscript (in the manner exemplified after the word 'footnote'[2] in this paragraph) immediately following that information or quotation. The footnotes[3] are numbered consecutively. At the bottom (the foot) of the page on which the superscript numbers appear, the writer presents the reader with enough information about the source so that the reader could access the sources himself, if he wanted to do so. The footnote[4] begins with the superscript number which is the same as the number in the text above, so the reader can easily match the reference in the text to the footnote[5] at the bottom of the page. The information in the footnote[6] will typically include the author's name, the title of the book or article or web site, the date the source was published, and the page number. Here are some examples of the kind of footnotes[7] you might include in your essay, if your teacher asks you to use the footnote[8] form of citation. Study them carefully and you will get a good idea of the kind of information you should include in your footnotes[9]. Note also that:

- Complete bibliographical information needs to be provided once. Subsequent footnotes to the same source may list just the author's last name and page number. Specify, as well, the work, if you have used more than one source from the same author.
- Book titles and journal titles are italicised. Article titles are in single quotation marks.
- If the author's name is mentioned in the text of the essay, it need not be repeated in the footnote.
- The bibliographical information in a footnote can be preceded or followed by commentary from the essay's author.

- More than one source can be cited in a single footnote if the same information is contained within more than one of the sources you consulted.

- If you cite a source from the Internet, include both the date of publication and the date you accessed the source.

[1]Mikhail Bakhtin, *Rabelais and his World,* trans. by Helene Iswolsky (Cambridge, MA: MIT Press, 1968), p. 48.

[2]Leonard Fitsimmons, 'Preserving the habitat of the Vancouver Island Marmot', *North American Journal of Endangered Species,* 24(1999), 78–91.

[3]*Romeo and Juliet,* ed. by W.S. Anderson (London: Parthenon, 1988), p. 76 (III, iv, 31–33). All quotations are from this edition.

[4]For an excellent discussion of this issue from a Marxist perspective see also W.W. Grayton, *Russian Economic Feudalism, 1900–1933* (New York: Pencil & Co., 1989).

[5]Johan Morton vigorously refutes evidence of Wilner's homosexuality. See his article, 'Persona and narrator in Evan Wilner's *Pride of the Great Plains*', in *Studies in Nineteenth Century Fiction,* 79(1998), 276–297.

[6]*Henry James: Letters,* ed. by Leon Edel, 4 vols (Cambridge, MA, and London: Harvard University Press, 1977–84), IV (1984), 650.

[7]Ben Wong, 'The real Vitamin C content in supermarket orange juice', *British Journal of Nutrition,* 57(1998), 7–16. Online. <http://www.bjnaompe.cvale.ca/durable> Accessed May 3, 1999.

For a complete discussion of the correct use of footnotes in academic writing, see *MHRA Style Book: Notes for Authors, Editors, and Writers of Theses* (5th edition). The MHRA is the Modern Humanities Research Association. Their style book is available from W.S. Maney & Sons Ltd., Hudson Road, Leeds LS9 7DL.

The References List at the end of the essay

Another method of citing sources correctly is to place, at the end of your essay, a list of the references you have used in your essay. The References List or Bibliography is organised alphabetically, according to the author's last name. If the source is anonymous, it is placed in the list alphabetically by its title.

Study carefully the following References List. Note that:

- The list is arranged alphabetically by the author's last name.
- Words in the titles of articles contained within books or journals are not capitalised, except for the first word, the first word in a subtitle, and proper nouns. Article titles are in normal (regular, or roman) font, enclosed in single quotation marks.
- Book titles are either italicised or underlined. The first and all important words in a book title are capitalised, while words such as 'and', 'or', 'the' remain in lower case.
- Words in journal titles are capitalised, and journal titles are underlined or placed in italics.
- Electronic sources include the online address and the date upon which the writer of the essay who is using the online source accessed the source. This date is necessary because authors of online articles can change the content of their articles after a researcher has read and used information from that source.

Bibliography

Arden, E. (1999). 'The politically-correct writer.' *Stringers Quarterly* [Online] *2.1*. Available: http://www/string_quart.bi.camduei/vol2.txt. [2000, March 9].

Burchfield, R. W. (1996). *The New Fowler's Modern English Usage*, 3rd ed. Oxford: Clarendon Press.

Clinton, W. (1998). 'State of the Union address.' January 27, 1998. Online. <http://www.pub.whitehouse.gov/urires/I2R?pdi://oma.eop.gov.us/1998/01/27/11.text.1>. [1999, February 24].

Davidson, T. & Aristos, J. (2000). *The Compact English Handbook* (2nd ed.). Birmingham: Zevon.

Hacker, D. (1998). *The Bedford Handbook*, 5th ed., Instructors Annotated Edition. Boston: Bedford.

Macher, Y. (1999). 'Keeping up with language variation.' *British Journal of Speech and Text Communication, 22,* 478–499.

Meyers, M.W. (1990). 'Current generic pronoun usage: An empirical study.' *American Speech, 65*, 1990, 228–237.

Readers must know the place in the text of the essay where the author of the essay is using information from a secondary source. In the References-list method, the author of the essay does this by placing the author's last name, the date the source was published, and the page number on which the quote or the information appears in parentheses immediately following the quote or the clip of information, for example: (Smith, 2001, p. 57). Note that commas follow the name and the year, and page is abbreviated. If the author's name is included in the text, then the year follows the author's name and the page number follows the information or the quote taken from the source. Here is an example:

> *Nevertheless, there is some support for this usage. Meyers (1990) examined the writing of 392 third and fourth-year university students, ranging in age from twenty-two to sixty-four and found that the use of 'they' and 'their' as singular pronouns is quite widespread. But grammar handbooks, usage guides, and most teachers will not sanction the use of the plural 'their' with a singular noun. Hacker (1998) uses this sentence – 'Every runner must train rigorously if they want to succeed' (p. 323) – as an example of an unacceptable use of the plural pronoun and recommends replacing 'their' with 'he or she' (p. 325).*

Note, again, the format of the citations in this passage. Note that if the author's name is mentioned in the text of the essay, it is not repeated in the parenthetical citation. Note that the date immediately follows the author's name. Note that the page number comes after the quote from the source. For the complete bibliographic information about these citations, the reader would go to the References List at the end of the essay. The reader would learn that the Meyers reference cites an article entitled 'Current generic pronoun usage: An empirical study', that the article was written by M.W. Meyers, that it was published in the volume 65, 1990 issue of *American Speech*, and that the article begins on page 228 and ends on page 237. Similarly, the reader would learn that the Hacker parenthetical citation references the fifth edition of a book by D. Hacker, entitled *The Bedford Handbook*, published by Bedford of Boston in 1998.

For a complete account of the References-List-with-Parenthetical-Citations Method of citing sources, consult the fourth edition of *The Publication Manual of the American Psychological Association.* This book can be ordered from the American Psychological Association, 750 First Street, NE, Washington, D.C., 20002-4242.

Our case study concluded

Audrey has to take just one more important step before she can submit her assignment. She must make absolutely certain she has cited the sources she has used in her essay accurately and completely, using the system prescribed by her professor.

Professor Fareed has asked her students to use the method for citing sources developed and prescribed by the Modern Language Association, the largest professional body for professors of language and literature. Audrey consults the MLA website at *www.mla.org* to get some information about citing sources; then she consults the book the website recommends: *The MLA Handbook for Writers of Research Papers*, 6th edition, by Joseph Gibaldi, 2003.

Here, then, is Audrey's list of works cited, which she appends to the last page of her essay to make it complete and ready for submission.

Works Cited

Booth, Stephen. 'Appendix I: Facts and theories about Shakespeare's sonnets.' *Shakespeare's Sonnets.* Ed. Stephen Booth. Yale University Press, 1977. 543–549.

Hecht, Anthony. 'Introduction.' *The Sonnets.* Ed. G. Blakemore Evans. Cambridge University Press, 1996. 7–28.

Hollander, John. 'Introduction.' *The Sonnets* (*The Pelican Shakespeare*). Ed. Stephen Orgel. New York, Penguin, 2001. xxiii–xlii.

Hubler, Edward. 'Shakespeare's sonnets and the commentators.' *The Riddle of Shakespeare's Sonnets.* New York: Basic Books, 1962. 1–22.

Hunt, Marvin. 'Be dark but not too dark: Shakespeare's Dark Lady as a sign of color.' *Shakespeare's Sonnets: Critical Essays.* Ed. James Schiffer. New York: Garland, 1999. 369–390.

Rowse, A.L. 'Introduction to the Third Edition.' *Shakespeare's Sonnets: A Modern Edition with Prose Versions, Introductions, and Notes.* 3rd ed. By A.L. Rowse. London: Macmillan Press, 1984. ix–xxv.

Sorenson, Cynthia. 'The grammar of the sonnets' dedication.' *The BardOnline* 2.1 (1996): n. pag. 8 Feb. 2003. *www.bardonlinev2n1/haynes/index.html.*

Wilson, Dover. 'Introduction.' *The Sonnets.* Ed. Dover Wilson. Cambridge University Press, 1969. xiii–cxxv.

Wilson, Katharine. *Shakespeare's Sugared Sonnets.* London: George Allen & Unwin, 1974.

Tutorial

Progress questions

1. What is a footnote? What information typically is included in a footnote?
2. What is a parenthetical citation? What information is typically included in a parenthetical citation?
3. What is a list of References? What information is typically included in a parenthetical citation?
4. What are the differences in format between a footnote and a source in a References List?

Discussion points

1. What is plagiarism? What steps must writers take to cite sources thoroughly and accurately?
2. What are the advantages and the disadvantages of the footnote method of citing sources and the parenthetical citation/reference list method?

Practical assignment

Research a topic of interest to you. Compile ten sources related to this topic: three books, five journal articles, and two Internet sources. Compose a References List citing these sources. Compose a list of footnotes citing these sources.

Study and revision tips

When you are making notes from a source that contains information you might incorporate into your essay, include in your notes the complete bibliographical information: author's full name, complete title of both article and journal or book, volume number and issue number, page numbers, place of publication, date of publication. You will not want to return to the library to find your source, if you have forgotten to record crucial information.

Ask your tutors, teachers, lecturers, instructors, professors what citation method they expect you to use in the essays you write for them.

Websites for Student Writers

If you want further information about the elements of good academic writing or if you want answers to specific questions about your writing, you can consult one of the many OWLS (Online Writing Labs) now available through the Internet. A comprehensive and annotated list of OWLS is available at:

http://www2.colgate.edu/diw/NWCAOWLS.html

There are scores of other online resources you can access which disseminate useful information about the rules of good writing. For students required to complete academic writing assignments in school, college, and university, the following web resources are among the best:

www.inkspot.com
www.columbia.edu/acis/bartleby/strunk
Gopher://Gopher.bgsu.edu:70/11/Departments/write
http://fur.rscc.cc.tn.us/cyberproject.html
http://www.dsu.edu/departments/liberal/cola/OWL
http://owl.english.purdue.edu/
http://www.rpi.edu/dept/11c/writecenter/web/home.html
http://www.trincoll.edu/writcent/aksmith.html
http://www.lsq.umich.edu/ecb/OWL/owl.html
http://www.missouri.edu/~writery

Index

academic voice, 127
acknowledging sources, 138
agreement, subject-verb, 79
analysis and interpretation, 33–38
apostrophe, 117

body paragraphs, 48

call number, 16
case study, 10–13, 19–22, 30–32, 62, 63, 68, 69, 130–126, 143, 144
cohesive ties, 65
collective noun as subject, 80
colon, 114
comma, 110
comma before a coordinate conjunction, 111
compare/contrast essay, 23, 25
concluding paragraph, 58–63
conclusion, 58–64
concrete words, 125
connotation, 124

dangling modifiers, 89
dash, 116
denotation, 124

ellipsis, 116
euphemism, 126
exclamation mark, 109

faulty parallelism, 91
footnote, 139
freewriting, 8
full stop, 109

generating ideas, 7

hyphen, 118

imperative mood, 78
indefinite pronoun as subject, 79
indicative mood, 78
informative mode, 4
internet, 18,19
irregular verbs, 76
it's and its, 75

jargon, 124

librarian, 19
literature review, 5

misplaced modifiers, 89–91

objective case, 72
opening paragraph, 39–44
ostentation language, 128

paragraph unity, 47
parallelism, 102
parentheses, 116
passive voice, 94
past participle, 76
period (see full stop) 109
periodic sentence, 104
periodical index, 17
periodicals, 17
persuasive mode, 6
planning an essay, 23–29

possessive case, 72
pronoun case, 72
pronoun/noun
  combination, 73
pronouns in a comparison,
  73
punctuation, 109–113

question mark, 109
questioning, 8
quotation marks, 115

readers, 1, 2, 3
reference list, 141
repetition and cohesion, 66
researching a topic, 15–17
run-on sentence, 87, 88

search engine, 18, 147
semi-colon, 109, 114
sentence fragment, 84–86
subjective case, 73
subject-verb agreement, 79
subjunctive mood, 78
subordination, 99–101
substitution and cohesion,
  67

thesis, 9, 10
thesis statement, 1, 9, 46
topic, 7
topic sentence, 46, 47
transition, 65
transitional words and
  phrases, 65

unity, 47

verb mood, 76
verb tense, 76

w5 strategy, 8
who and whom, 74
wordiness, 92–94